Do you happen to have a hedgerow abundant with wild food, some failed cabbages in your vegetable garden, a crop of edible weeds in flower bed, the sad remains of a joint, or just a solitary tin of pilchards in your cupboard? If you do, then there's a recipe here for you. It is the concept of making nourishing and enticing dishes with the cheapest of foods, from whatever source, which gives this unusual book its special value.

There are recipes for dishes throughout the seasons and the book includes not only tit-bits of advice, such as how to cook in a haybox and bottle fruit without buying preserving jars, but also humorous asides of the kind that will be familiar to readers of Elizabeth West's HOVEL IN THE HILLS and GARDEN IN THE HILLS.

With a commonsense attitude to metric conversion, and a light-hearted but informative introduction to each section, Elizabeth West has produced a book which will delight all cooks – not least those who enjoy an entertaining browse between meals.

Also by Elizabeth West

HOVEL IN THE HILLS
GARDEN IN THE HILLS
SUFFER LITTLE CHILDREN
and published by Corgi Books

Kitchen in the Hills
The Hovel Cookbook

Elizabeth West

CORGI BOOKS

KITCHEN IN THE HILLS
A CORGI BOOK 0 552 12072 3

Originally published in Great Britain by
Faber and Faber Ltd.

PRINTING HISTORY
Faber and Faber edition published 1981
Corgi edition published 1983
Corgi edition reprinted 1987

This book is set in 10/11 Mallard

Corgi Books are published by Transworld Publishers
Ltd., 61–63 Uxbridge Road, Ealing, London W5 5SA, in
Australia by Transworld Publishers (Aust.) Pty. Ltd.,
15–23 Helles Avenue, Moorebank, NSW 2170, and in New
Zealand by Transworld Publishers (N.Z.) Ltd., Cnr. Moselle
and Waipareira Avenues, Henderson, Auckland.

Printed and bound in Great Britain by
Cox & Wyman Ltd., Reading, Berks.

Contents

Introduction

'A *what*?' said Alan. 'A cookery book,' I replied. 'I'm going to write one. It will have cheap, honest-to-goodness recipes for people like us who haven't got much money.' He was silent for a moment. 'I would have thought,' he said cautiously, 'that writers of cookery books should, in the first case, be able to *cook*!'

From a man who eats up everything I put in front of him and often looks around for second helpings, such a comment can be dismissed as typical husband-like sarcasm and wouldn't be worth recording, except perhaps that it does make me examine my qualifications for producing such a book. I was once employed as a temporary relief professional cook (albeit by employers so incompetent in the kitchen themselves and so desperate for help that they would have considered taking on an intelligent gorilla), but I would prefer to offer as justification my long-practised ability to make the housekeeping money stretch, and to produce tasty and nourishing meals out of the cheapest ingredients. Alan wouldn't argue with any of this, but when I first put forward the idea of this book he argued a lot. 'To begin with,' he said in his usual wet-blanket manner, 'I'm not convinced that you know what you're doing. For instance—what's the weight of the onion you have in that pan?' (I was making soup and I hadn't the remotest idea of the weight of the onion.) 'Oh, I shall just say "one large onion",' I offered airily. 'What's a large onion?' he persisted. 'Your Uncle Bert grows them weighing up to 2 lb each . . . and another

7

thing, I don't suppose you know how much water you have put in the pan.' 'I shall say "dice the vegetables and cover with water",' I said. 'Which will just prove that you are telling lies,' he came back, 'because you can't cover diced vegetables with water. They float. I can see that you're going to produce the sort of book that I would throw across the room.'

Having torn my idea to shreds and convinced me that I was totally incompetent for the job, Alan then started to pick up the pieces and re-examine them. 'This book of yours,' he said a few days later (when I had abandoned all such plans and was thinking of writing short stories for children), 'provided I keep an eye on what you're doing, you shouldn't make too bad a mess of it. And you must include some of your pudding recipes—and that tasty thing you do with lentils in a casserole' . . . and so it was that *Kitchen in the Hills* started to take shape.

Having lived in happy, self-inflicted poverty for most of our married life, we are both in a strong position to advise on how to feed yourself well with the minimum of cost, but undoubtedly our attitudes of waste-not-want-not are inherited ones. Both of us came from working-class homes where money was in short supply, food was plain, and the menu repetitive.

I remember that my mother made soup on Tuesdays. The leftover bone from the weekend roast was boiled up with great lumps of swede and parsnip along with onions and pearl barley. This, with potatoes and dumplings, was midday dinner. Anything left in the saucepan was mashed up, watered down, and dished out with pieces of bread for our supper. We loved it. If, through reasons of childish pig-headedness, any of us were disinclined to finish up the saucepan of soup that same evening we were reminded of all those poor starving children who had to make do with 'kettle broth' for their supper. I knew all about those poor starving children. I had a picture of them in one of my books. They were thin, barefoot, with ragged clothes and straight hair, and they were bunched around a window looking at the scene within where a group of plump children with curly hair and in party dress were whooping it up around a table loaded with jellies and cakes. As I sat at home smugly spooning up my soup in the warm security of the living room I gained a sneaky satisfaction from the thought of those ragged children who were probably outside right now, beyond the drawn curtains, pressing their noses against the window and trying to get a whiff of my soup. It wasn't until I was a little older and able to compare notes with other children whose fathers had cars and who had carpets in their homes (my father went to work on a bike and the only floor covering in our house was lino and mats) that I came to realize that poverty was relative. But I didn't find out about kettle broth until I met Alan.

Although his early childhood was spent in conditions of respectable penury, he has cosy fireside memories similar to mine—and kettle broth is one of them. He particularly remembers winter evenings. Warm and snug after his bath in the galvanized tub in front of the fire, he would sit on a stool in his pyjamas watching his mother. She would lift the kettle from the fire and half-fill a small pudding basin with hot water. Then came the ritual sprinkling of pepper and salt and, on particularly hungry days, a few broken crusts of bread would be added. This was his supper and, hugging the warm bowl to his knees, he would tuck into it with solemn relish. Kettle broth was obviously a good idea. It was filling, there was a savoury illusion created by the seasoning, and it sent him to bed with something warm in his belly. He remembers it with affection.

But we grew up in a rapidly changing world, and by the time we married things were different. The working classes had new clothes, cars, holidays abroad, and expectations of a non-stop acquisition of possessions (usually referred to as 'a better standard of living'). But we hadn't been married for long before we

9

began to question this way of life and to look around for a better one. We found it at Hafod.

Hafod is a small, isolated and primitive holding high on the moors of Dinbych in North Wales. We bought it in 1964 and came to understand about things like storms, blizzards and floods, and we also discovered how to find food in the wilderness—and how to grow our own alongside it. The one problem we never solved was how to make money, and our thirteen years at Hafod were passed in a financially hand-to-mouth manner which kept us well below the 'bread-line'. We earned money by carrying out odd jobs, which was totally satisfactory when work was available locally, but not so good when we had to travel further afield in order to find it. Sometimes we had to shut up the cottage for weeks at a stretch, and each time this happened we hated it. We hated the final shutting of the front door, the checking around the outbuildings and the locking of the front gate. So this going-away-to-earn-money was a bogy we tried to ignore for as long as possible. We kept our money in a little brass bowl on the sideboard, and we made that money last as long as possible. There was always food available from the garden. In spring, summer and autumn I could wander out of doors and find roots, herbs, leaves or fruit from which to make a meal. In winter we had our stores of root crops, pulses and bottled fruit and chutney. So long as we had some flour, oatmeal and cheese in stock we wouldn't starve—and I made sure that the flour, oatmeal and cheese stretched as far as possible. Only when the brass bowl was empty would we consider going away for work. Whilst it might have been possible to continue to survive by drinking spring water and feeding from our roots and herbs, we also wanted things like tea, coffee, honey, and Alan's tobacco—never mind such things as paying the rates and buying a National Insurance stamp.

The ups and downs of our life at Hafod have been

described in my previous books,* and it was during this era that my making-the-most-of-what-you've-got cooking skills developed into something approaching an art form: wild foods, cultivated foods, canned and fresh shop foods—I scoured the moorland, the hedgerows, the woods, garden and the supermarket to find food that was free, or cheap and nourishing. I produced dishes that were satisfying and tasty . . . and we thrived on them. During our years in the wilderness we had no illness; not even the slightest cough or cold.

Nevertheless, perhaps Alan is right in his claim that I'm not a *real* cook. He knows my limitations. Ask me to prepare the food for a dinner party and I would get into such a panic that the food would be burnt or underdone, and certainly wouldn't look right. Even one of my well-tried cake recipes will go wrong if I'm trying to produce it for guests, and I am certainly incapable of producing any exquisitely delicate pastries, confectioneries, or dainty gâteaux.

I once tried to show off with my orange butter-cream cake (recipe no. 243). I had made one that had turned out particularly well. The cake was light and soft and had risen evenly. The butter cream was rich and tasty, and the orange-flecked icing on top was smooth and attractive. It seemed too good to attack with the knife. Then I heard that my neighbour Gwen was ill, so I decided to take the cake across to her as a present. We hadn't been at Hafod long, and I didn't know Gwen very well, but I sometimes bought eggs from their farm, which was about a mile along the lane from us. Although they were in a position on the moor more isolated even than ours they had recently been connected to the mains electricity supply (we produced our own by means of a wind-charger), and I was admittedly curious to see how this link-up with civilization might have changed her kitchen.

I decided to take a short cut across the moor—

* *Hovel in the Hills* and *Garden in the Hills*.

11

forgetting that, although we can in fact see their farm from our hillside, a fast-flowing river lies between us and them. I placed my cake in a basket, covered it with a nice white cloth, and set off. I felt curiously prim and old-fashioned. I was setting off, on foot, upon an errand of neighbourly good will, and in this timeless moorland landscape it seemed a much more appropriate action than, say, a 'phone call or a 'get-well' card. The afternoon was hot. Larks spiralled dizzily upwards, singing in sweet, non-stop ecstasy. The bleating of sheep came faintly from the distance, and an occasional curlew gave a sad short cry—too drowsy with summer warmth to fill the air with its full lament. Heather and ling scratched at my ankles and I wished that I'd changed into boots. Then I came to the first fence. I had forgotten about the fences. Newly repaired with gleaming barbed wire, this first one sloped across the moor each way from where I stood hopelessly looking at it, wearing my silly sandals and summer dress. I had to follow the fence for about half a mile before I found a gateway. Fortunately the second fence was in poor condition and easily negotiable—but then I came to the river. By now I was hot, scratched, sweaty, and going off the whole idea. Another detour of about a quarter of a mile brought me to a place where I could ford the stream by stone-hopping, but although I kept my feet dry in this operation, the exertion broke one of my sandal straps. I hobbled the remaining half-mile to Gwen's farm, but it wasn't until I was approaching the yard that I thought to look at the cake. I peered cautiously under the cloth, and was alarmed to see that in the heat of the afternoon the top half had slewed sideways over the butter-cream filling. I gently edged it back into position, but then cursed myself for leaving a grimy fingerprint on the rapidly softening iced top. As I loped the remaining few yards to Gwen's back door I noted how deserted the yard seemed. The tractor was in its shed, the car was parked on the cobbles, and the dogs were creating a snarling, scrabbling furious din inside the cowshed. But no one was around. The back door was firmly shut, and there was no sign of human life anywhere. There was no answer to my first knock, I banged a bit harder, and then again. Finally I heard someone at the door, and Gwen opened it. She was in her best dress, her hair had been recently permed and, apart from a slightly flushed face, she looked perfectly healthy to me. Without having given it any conscious thought I had been expecting to find her wrapped in shawls, sitting coughing in front of the fire, and I imagined her holding out grateful trembling hands to receive my delicious cake to cheer her lonely afternoon. From the noise I could hear coming from the kitchen behind her I could tell that she certainly wasn't lonely. I was wishing more than ever that I hadn't come.

Gwen was delighted to see me. Oh yes, she was better now, thank you, which was just as well because today was her birthday, and I must come in and see her present from the family.

I shall always remember the scene that followed in the kitchen. The new television set in the corner —going full blast when I arrived—was politely turned off, and the assembled group of friends, relatives and children rearranged themselves reluctantly to allow my entry. 'Time we all had tea,' said Gwen, throwing back the heavy chenille curtains that had been shutting out the sunlight, and there in front of the window was a table loaded with trifles, jellies, plates piled with buttered Bara Brith and, in the middle, a large birthday cake, exquisitely iced with fancy trellis work and decorated with pink roses and candles. 'I've brought you another cake, ha, ha, ha,' I said, hearty in my embarrassment (there was no hiding it now—Gwen had been eyeing my basket ever since I had come in). 'Just thought you might not have enough to eat, ho, ho, ho.' No one else laughed. They were all staring expectantly at my basket. I handed it to Gwen. She removed the cloth and peered in. 'That's nice,' she said, trying

13

awkwardly to lift the cake. Her thumb sank into the icing as she manoeuvred the cake past the basket handle, 'I'll just go and get a plate.' But then it happened. The top half of the cake, slithering oozily on its butter-cream filling, slipped from under her thumb and fell to the floor. There were clucks of consolation from everyone as Gwen bustled about trying to remove the cake from the mat. 'Such a pity—nice cake too, really—I like soft icing, don't you?—nice for a change.' A plate was found; the cake was reassembled and, the remains of its iced top decorated with a coconut-matting imprint, a few dog's hairs and an assortment of fingerprints, it took its place on the table.

I don't make orange butter-cream cake very often. Being one of my least economical recipes it is reserved for 'special occasions' (our own occasions only—since the fiasco in Gwen's kitchen I've not made one for anybody else) but, even with the cost of the orange, eggs and butter, it is less than half the price of any similar cake that you might buy, and the ingredients are pure and good to eat.

I think you will find that this concept of economy plus nourishment is reflected throughout the book; although we no longer live in the hills, we are still short of money, and the dishes tried and tested over twenty years of married life are still serving us well.

So here you are ... one woman's collection of recipes; some of them adapted war-time ones, passed on to me from my mother; some from old friends; some from new friends, and some my own concoctions brought from the wilderness. All of them will produce dishes that are cheap and good to eat. What's more (by now you will have gathered that I am the humblest of cooks) you will find them easy to prepare.

Sorting through these recipes took longer than I thought because I kept getting side-tracked. All those scraps of paper covered with different handwritings brought back too many memories of old friends and long-gone eras, but strangely enough, the recipes I found most difficult to write out concisely were my own concoctions. 'Put breadcrumbs in a bowl' I wrote when describing my mixed herb stuffing, 'then add pepper and salt. Sprinkle in the sage, thyme and marjoram, and finally add the grated onion.' Fortunately Alan was checking the script behind me. His pencil went through the lot. 'Mix together all ingredients' he scrawled.

Alan has been hovering at my shoulder throughout the creation of this book—both at the stove and the typewriter. He wanted to make sure that I wrote down what I *actually did*, which is just as well, because I'm the sort of cook who adds a bit of this, or a sprinkle of that, without really knowing the amounts involved.

But now the job is done, and all my most useful recipes have been assembled in some sort of order. Now, when I want to make Mrs Lloyd's gingerbread, I don't have to go scrabbling through a drawer full of tea towels, skewers, polythene bags, foil, jam-jar lids and out-of-date '5p-off-special-offer' coupons in order to find the envelope on which Mrs Lloyd wrote it. I simply consult Alan's index.

I can see I'm going to find this book most useful—and I hope that you will too.

Some Facts and Figures

METRICATION

The probability of the metric system being here to stay doesn't stop a large number of us ignoring it. I have yet to find a butcher prepared to sell me 250 grammes of minced beef, and I know of one large departmental store that has gone back to yards and inches in its curtain department, having given up the battle with customers who refused to think in metres. I still ask for a 3-lb bag of flour and $\frac{1}{2}$ lb of margarine—and it is of but academic interest to me that the flour is labelled 1·5 kg and the margarine 250 g.

As an old fashioned imperial woman with no leanings whatsoever towards the metric scales, the problem of converting my recipes has required a lot of hard (and I hope logical) thought. Most cookery books use the conversion of 25 grammes = 1 ounce. As the metric scale encourages us to think in round numbers—100, 250, 500, etc.—and we will want to divide these figures into halves and quarters, this desire to make 1 ounce equal 25 grammes is understandable. But in fact 1 ounce is not 25 grammes—and as the weight increases so does the error. So we are faced with a conversion table that tries to persuade us that whereas 1 ounce equals 25 grammes and 4 ounces equal 100 grammes, 8 ounces is obliged to equal 250 grammes! Having been brought up to believe that 1 + 1 = 2, my brain suffers a short circuit when faced with this sort of arithmetical boggle—especially when I know that the 250 grammes of margarine referred to above in fact weighs nearly 9 ounces on my kitchen scales. So I have decided to say that 1 ounce equals 30 grammes. I am well aware that 1 ounce does not equal 30 grammes; it equals (officially) 28·35 grammes. But I know for a fact that my kitchen scales are incapable of registering the difference of that 1·65 grammes—and probably yours are too.

For the same reason of comparative accuracy I have decided not to say that 1 pint equals $\frac{1}{2}$ litre, but to convert the liquid measure into decilitres. For the purposes of this book, therefore:

1 ounce avoirdupois (oz) = 30 grammes (g)
1 pint imperial (pt) = 6 decilitres (dl)

By using these conversion factors you can increase or decrease the quantities as much as you like without running into difficulties (e.g. as 1 oz = 30 g, so 16 oz = 480 g). What is more you can if you wish (although I can see no reason why you should!) mix imperial and metric weights and measures in the same recipe. The discrepancies are so slight (less than 1 oz in the pound) that it won't make any difference. (If you don't believe this, just consider for a moment the quantities involved in, say, a gingerbread (following recipe no. 227) that you might want to make for a church fête. If you increased the quantities tenfold and used 1 lb 14 oz margarine to 1,800 g flour, the overweight of flour incurred by using the metric quantity would be just over 3 oz on 3 lb 12 oz. I don't think your gingerbread would suffer as a result of this.)

OTHER MEASUREMENTS

Teaspoon (tsp)	imperial or	Slightly rounded
Dessertspoon (dsp)	metric	(With treacle and
Tablespoon (tbsp)	standard	golden syrup I have
		assumed that you
		will have almost as
		much below the
		spoon as above it)

OVEN TEMPERATURES

No oven temperatures are quoted in my recipes. I have used the expressions 'very slow, slow, moderate, moderately hot, and hot'. This is because, although I have cooked with solid fuels, oil, gas and electricity, I have no experience of cooking on stoves that have numbered knobs or scales. Indeed, my present stove doesn't even carry a helpful thermometer with the words 'slow, mod. or hot' on it; I have come to understand the idiosyncracies of my oven by trial and error, and judge my cooking times accordingly. I suspect that in fact most women 'know' their own oven and that my descriptions of oven heats are sufficient. However, as a *rough guide only* I give below a table of comparative temperatures.

Oven Heat	Degrees Fahrenheit	Regulo Mark	Degrees Celsius
Very slow	200		(95) 100
	225	$\frac{1}{4}$	110
Slow	250	$\frac{1}{2}$	120 130
	275	1	
Moderate			140
	300	2	150
	325	3	160
	350	4	170
			180
	375	5	190
			200

Oven Heat	Degrees Fahrenheit	Regulo Mark	Degrees Celsius
Moderately hot	{ 400	6	
	425		210
		7	220
Hot	{ 450		230
			240
	475	8	(245)

(The figures in brackets are not usually marked on cookers)

SLOW COOKING

My occasional instruction to 'cook overnight in a very slow oven' will present no problem to readers who have heat retention cookers, or cookers with a special low setting, but to those who haven't I recommend the use of an electric casserole.

My electric casserole uses 115 watts of electricity on the low setting and 160 watts on the high setting (comparable to the amount used by a light bulb), and can safely be left on overnight, or whilst I am away from home all day. The first casserole I bought was faulty. The glazed surface became crazed after its first use, the pot always retained the odour of the dish previously cooked, and if left unused for a few days a mould developed on the surface. I complained to the manufacturers and they sent me a free replacement. This replacement casserole has proved to be satisfactory.

However, being concerned at the possible bacteriological hazards of cooking food at low temperatures for long periods, I wrote to the Central Public Health Laboratory for an opinion and received a reply from Diane Roberts (Senior Microbiologist of the Food Hygiene Laboratory) who very kindly sent me a copy of her article on the subject which appeared in the magazine *Environmental Health*.* The article, describing tests carried out upon chicken with stuffing, breast of lamb with stuffing, and steak and kidney—all cooked in a slow electric casserole—concludes with the following paragraph:

'It would appear from the experiments carried out that the hazards of using the electric casserole are no greater than those from conventional cooking methods providing the manufacturers' instructions are followed. It is extremely important that the food is either eaten hot immediately or removed from the casserole, cooled rapidly and refrigerated.'

However, there were no such reassurances from the Public Health Laboratory Service on another form of slow cooking—haybox cookery. Diane Roberts was dubious about the whole idea, especially with regard to cooking meats. Nevertheless, haybox cookery has been around for a long time now. I have a book of haybox recipes. It was published in 1939; it is rather vague and woolly and contains all sorts of unlikely and dodgy-sounding ideas. Yet so-called hayboxes were used by the Military Services during the last war, and a friend of ours spent her childhood on a farm where the use of the haybox was a regular part of their domestic routine, with no ill effects so far as she recalls. There is currently a revival of interest in this form of cooking, and in a recently published book on self-sufficiency mention was made of a 'hot-box' that was available on the retail market.

As the idea of getting something for nothing is appealing, Alan and I decided to experiment with our own version of the haybox. We used a large cardboard box, measuring approximately 24 in (60 cm) × 15 in (37½ cm) × 12 in (30 cm) and stuffed it with old clothes (wool, cotton and synthetics). I had soaked overnight

* 'Slow Cooking with an Electrical Casserole. Results of Bacteriological Tests', *Environmental Health*, October 1977, p 214.

5 oz (150 g) of butter beans. In the morning I put them into a 2-pt (12-dl) cast-iron saucepan, three-quarters filled the pan with water and brought them to the boil. I let them simmer for about two minutes and then transferred the saucepan to a prepared 'well' amongst the old clothes in our 'haybox'. More old clothes were rammed on top and the box was covered with a tea tray lid which was weighted down with the flour bin. When I came home from work that evening I found that the butter beans were *perfectly cooked*, and the water was slightly warm. I only had to bring the pan to the boil in order to serve the beans with the boiled bacon, baked potatoes, cauliflower and parsley sauce that we were having for dinner. (The butter beans would otherwise have needed three hours' cooking in the electric casserole.) We have tried a vegetable casserole dish with similarly successful results. But I would not contemplate using a haybox for cooking meat. For one thing I don't think that it would work, but also, like Diane Roberts, I am 'dubious'.

RECIPE INGREDIENTS

My recipes are all of an adaptable variety, and the quantities quoted are not critical. Even in the bread, biscuits, cake and preserves sections you can give or take an ounce, and in the meat and vegetable sections the recipes can be adapted to suit what you happen to have. I would like to think that this book supplied you with a few basic ideas that you can change or improve upon as you desire.

I have assumed that all ingredients are ready for use, i.e.:

Meat: washed, and any unwanted fat and gristle removed.

Fish: washed, gutted where necessary, and head, tail and fins removed.

21

Dried fruit: washed and stemmed.

Vegetables and fresh fruit: washed (and peeled and cored where necessary); dried pulses picked over and foreign objects removed (I frequently find tiny stones amongst my lentils). Where I have quoted onions you can use shallots instead if you wish. Wild foods (leaves, berries, fungi and nuts) appear occasionally throughout the book. I saw no reason to put them in a special section because I gather them with and use them alongside the foods I pick from my garden or buy from shops.

Herbs: we both love herbs, in spite of hailing from working class families who were a little suspicious of them. Alan remembers that his mother garnished food with sprigs of parsley which were normally left at the side of the plate. Upon his enquiry 'Can I eat it?' his mother replied, 'You can if you like.' This struck him as a very unsatisfactory answer, and one which left him doubtful about parsley for many years. Similarly, I remember that my mother grew beautiful sage bushes, but our Christmas chicken was always stuffed with something out of a packet labelled 'Paxo'. This suspicion of herbs still abounds. I recently had lunch in a country hotel with a colleague who wasn't at all happy at my choice from the menu of Herb Omelette. 'You'll probably find it contains things they've picked from outside the back door!' he hissed. His own choice was gazpacho soup and goulash. '*I* like to know what I'm eating,' was his confident declaration.

Herbs are now part of our way of life—and wherever we live we must grow them. Even if I were limited to a few square feet of garden space I would grow herbs—rosemary, sage, mint, thyme, marjoram and parsley, for these are my favourites. During the early summer I pick large bunches of all herbs (except parsley) to dry for use in the winter. (Parsley usually survives green and cheerful throughout the year—I have even fumbled for it beneath the snow.) Many people prefer to preserve mint by making up jars of mint jelly or sauce, but I think this is an unnecessary labour when mint dries perfectly well, and a few leaves can be so easily crumbled into vinegar and sugar when a little mint sauce is needed. Admittedly the leaves become rather brown and un-mint-like in appearance, but as soon as they are mixed with the vinegar quite a presentable mint sauce appears—and it tastes almost as good as fresh mint. Where I have suggested 'mixed dried herbs' in my recipes I have left you to decide on the mixture. Generally speaking, my own preference is for two parts thyme to one part each of marjoram and sage. (With fish dishes I like to use *lemon* thyme, or balm.) If fresh herbs are used instead of dried herbs, then roughly three times the bulk quantity is needed.

Canned foods: I consider canned foods to be emergency rations, and at Hafod, at the start of winter, we had always to be prepared for emergencies. The storms of winter could blanket us in snow for weeks on end, making it impossible to get to the village shop, except on foot and even then with difficulty. By the autumn my store cupboard shelves would be loaded with home-produced jams, bottled fruit, chutney and sauces, and to these would be added flour, oatmeal, various dried pulses and canned foods such as meat, fish, baked beans, tomatoes and milk. By the following summer I would like to have used up any remaining canned food, and I have included in this book some of the dishes I concocted for this purpose.

Seasoning: pepper: except where otherwise stated, I use freshly ground black pepper.

Salt: we use iodized table salt. With most dishes, where salt is desired, I use very little in cooking as we prefer to add it at the table, and I never boil vegetables with salt. For one thing I don't like the way it affects cooking pots, and for another I like to use the vegetable water (flavoured with yeast extract) to make gravy, or as a pre-dinner drink.

Yeast (or meat) extracts: Alan and I are Marmite fans. Several supermarkets sell their own brands of yeast extract which are quite satisfactory—and also cheaper. (Possibly only Marmite purists like Alan can tell the difference. He even adds it to his home-brewed beer!) If you have a favourite brand of yeast extract (or even meat extract) then obviously it may be used instead of Marmite.

Suet: fresh suet (bought from the butcher in a lump) is best. If chopped and lightly floured and salted it will keep for many months. However, pre-packed 'granulated' suet is a satisfactory alternative.

Breadcrumbs: all breadcrumbs referred to in the recipes are *soft*.

Sugar: unless otherwise stated the 'sugar' referred to in all recipes is white granulated sugar. When 'brown sugar' is mentioned any sort of brown sugar may be used, but preferably cane sugar such as Barbados or demerara rather than something vaguely labelled 'soft light' or 'dark' brown sugar.

BOILED PUDDINGS

When tied in a cloth: pour boiling water over a clean cotton cloth, then wring and cover one side with flour (sprinkled fairly thickly). Place pudding on floured side and roll up, allowing room for pudding to expand. Tie both ends with one piece of string so that the connecting length forms a handle.

When cooked in a basin: well grease the basin. The pudding mixture should not fill it—about 1 in (25 mm) should be left for expansion during cooking. Cover with aluminium foil or lid (some basins have special clip-on lids). Alternatively use grease-proof paper and cover with a piece of thin cotton cloth (I use a piece of old pillow slip) tied around the lip with string. (Fat

24

wrappers can be used under the cloth if you don't mind
the coloured imprint of 'Blogg's Best Butter' coming out
on top of your boiled pudding.) Place a piece of folded
cotton cloth in the bottom of the saucepan so that the
pudding basin doesn't overheat nor jiggle noisily when
boiling. The water in the saucepan should be kept
topped up to about three-quarters full.

RECIPE TITLES

I know that many of my recipe titles will mean little to
you. You couldn't possibly visualize Dan Hayman who
gave me the recipe for Brack; you haven't the privilege
of knowing Aunt Daisy, and you probably have to guess
at the pronunciation of Stwnch and Brwyes. But they
are all of great significance to me and so I have
included them. However, common sense rules in the
index. Each recipe has been indexed by a sensible
description of the dish, and not necessarily by its title
in the book.

SERVINGS

Where appropriate, I have suggested the approximate
number of people each recipe should serve—but I am
assuming that something else will accompany the dish.
Very few serving suggestions have been included
because, if you are anything like me, you will serve
each dish with what you happen to have in stock. In the
case of vegetable additions I would serve what was
currently available from the garden. And if, say, we
have plenty of purple-sprouting broccoli but everything else was a bit behind, then we would eat purple-
sprouting broccoli every day until the other crops were
ready for picking.

1. Soup

1. Clear Vegetable Soup
2. Thick Vegetable Soup
3. Vegetable and Oatmeal Soup
4. Broad Bean Soup
5. Cabbage Soup
6. Cabbage and Bacon Soup
7. Cabbage and Ham-bone Soup
8. Carrot and Oatmeal Soup
9. Carrot and Onion Soup
10. Chestnut Soup
11. Jerusalem Artichoke Soup
12. Leaf and Bacon (Hungry Gap) Soup
13. Lettuce Cream Soup
14. Lettuce and Weed Soup
15. Nettle and Vegetable Soup
16. Onion Soup
17. Onion and Potato Soup
18. Parsnip and Onion Soup
19. Pea Pod Soup
20. Potato Cole (February) Soup
21. Tomato and Onion Soup
22. Vegetable Marrow Soup
23. Butter Bean and Tomato Soup
24. Haricot Bean and Tomato Soup
25. Dried Pea Soup
26. Dried Pea and Lettuce Soup
27. Lentil Soup
28. Lentil and Vegetable Soup
29. Bread Soup
30. Bone Soup
31. Pig's Head Soup

A bowl of soup with a hunk of crusty wholemeal bread is almost a meal in itself, and once you have become 'soup-minded' you will find that no usable leftovers are wasted (pea pods, turnip tops and even weeds can be used). So long as you have some vegetables and herbs —and maybe some dripping—you can rustle up a light, nourishing meal. And the unmistakable tastiness of soups made from fresh vegetables will persuade you that it's worth making them yourself. On a cold winter's night a bowl of home-made soup will comfort and delight—and if you search your garden carefully it can be made for next to nothing.

At Hafod our diet was very much influenced by the seasons. In winter our soups were made from root vegetables and dried pulses, but as soon as plants stirred to life in the spring I was out in the garden gathering chickweed and chives to cook with a few chopped kale leaves. During the summer and autumn the flavours and textures of our soups changed subtly, with the inclusion of lettuce, nettles and fresh herbs; then winter found me sorting out my dried peas and haricot beans once more.

The following recipes are a selection of Hafod soups—but almost any combination of leaf or root vegetable would be worth trying—and if you happen to have some stock to use, instead of water, so much the better. One of the cheapest and tastiest sources of good stock is a meaty hambone. I know of a grocer who cures massive joints of ham from which he carves delicious and expensive slices to sell to his wealthier customers—knowing that when the last full slice has been lifted from the joint, one of his poorer customers (like me) will come along to buy the bone for about 80p. There are always great chunks of meat at both ends, and from the last one I bought I hacked off about $1\frac{1}{2}$ lb (720 g) of ham to use with salads before putting the bone (still with plenty of meat attached) into a casserole with vegetables to make a tasty and nourishing stew which lasted us for 2 days. Alternatively I could have removed all meat from the bone before boiling, and used the stock for any of the following bean, pea or cabbage soups (see particularly recipe no. 7). Another good source of stock is a pig's head. At the time of writing half a pig's head costs around 60p. From this you can get a large pudding basin full of brawn (recipe no. 75); the basic stock for a good soup (recipe no. 31) plus a small basin of pork dripping. No matter how much inflation has soared by the time you are reading this, you are not likely to find anything of better value in your butcher's shop.

The proportions given in my recipes will provide a generous bowl of soup for two hungry people, or a 'polite' serving for four or five people who are expecting something else as well. Where no seasoning has been suggested, this is because we prefer to add pepper and salt at the table. (You will certainly need no salt if yeast extract has been included, nor if a hambone has been used for stock.)

1. Clear Vegetable Soup   Serves 4

sufficient raw vegetable leftovers, in good condition, and chopped, to three-quarters fill a large saucepan (e.g. outside cabbage leaves and stalks, pea pods, leek trimmings, celery tops, turnip tops, old lettuces, etc.)
1 oz (30 g) dripping
6 oz (180 g) onion, unpeeled and sliced
1 clove garlic, unpeeled and sliced
2 tbsps chopped chives
2 tbsps chopped parsley
$\frac{1}{2}$ tsp yeast extract

Melt dripping in a saucepan and fry onions and garlic gently for a few minutes. Add all other ingredients except chives, parsley and yeast extract. Cover with about $1\frac{1}{2}$ pts (9 dl) water and simmer for 1 hour. Strain and discard vegetables. Stir chives, parsley and yeast extract into soup and simmer for 1 minute.

2. Thick Vegetable Soup   *Serves 4*

1 lb (480 g) mixed
   vegetables, including
   onions, shallots or
   garlic, all cut small
1 oz (30 g) pearl barley
   or rice

1 oz (30 g) dripping
2 tbsps chopped parsley
1 tsp yeast extract
pepper

Simmer all ingredients in 1 pt (6 dl) water in a sauce-pan (with lid on) for $1\frac{1}{2}$ to 2 hours. Stir occasionally, and add more water if necessary.

3. Vegetable and Oatmeal Soup   *Serves 4*

1 lb (480 g) mixed
   vegetables, including
   onions, chopped
2 tbsps oatmeal (or
   4 tbsps rolled oats)

1 oz (30 g) dripping
1 tsp mixed dried herbs
$\frac{1}{4}$ pt ($1\frac{1}{2}$ dl) milk
salt, pepper
a little cheese, grated

Melt dripping in a saucepan and fry oatmeal gently for a few minutes, stirring continuously. Add $1\frac{1}{2}$ pts (9 dl) water, bring to the boil, add vegetables and herbs, season and simmer for 1 hour. Add milk and bring to the boil again, then stir in cheese.

4. Broad Bean Soup   *Serves 4*

This is a good way of using up old and tough beans.

12oz (360 g) shelled
   broad beans
1 shallot

$\frac{1}{2}$ oz (15 g) butter
salt, pepper
$\frac{1}{2}$ pt (3 dl) milk

Boil beans with shallot in 1 pt (6 dl) water in a saucepan for about 30 minutes. Drain and keep liquor. Remove skins from beans, then mash with shallot and butter. Return liquor to pan with mash, bring to the boil and simmer for 15 minutes, then stir in seasoning and milk and re-heat.

5. Cabbage Soup
Serves 4

$\frac{1}{2}$ small cabbage,
   shredded and
   chopped
8 oz (240 g) potatoes,
   diced
$\frac{1}{2}$ oz (15 g) butter
1 clove garlic, chopped

$\frac{1}{2}$ oz (15 g) plain flour
$\frac{1}{2}$ tsp grated nutmeg
$\frac{1}{4}$ pt (1 $\frac{1}{2}$ dl) milk
salt, pepper
2 oz (60 g) cheese,
   grated

Simmer cabbage and potatoes in 1 pt (6 dl) water in a saucepan until tender (about 20 minutes). In a saucepan of similar size melt butter and fry garlic gently for a few minutes, then stir in flour. Remove from heat and slowly add liquor from cabbage and potatoes, stirring continuously. Add nutmeg, then simmer for 15 minutes. Pour into cabbage and potato mixture. Stir in milk, season, bring to the boil, then stir in cheese.

6. Cabbage and Bacon Soup
Serves 4

$\frac{1}{2}$ small cabbage,
   shredded and
   chopped
4 rashers streaky
   bacon, chopped

1 oz (30 g) dripping
2 tbsps rice
salt, pepper
2 tsbps chopped parsley

Melt dripping in a saucepan and fry bacon for 5 minutes, then add cabbage. Toss it around, put lid on and cook slowly for about 10 minutes. Add about 1 pt (6 dl) water and stir in rice. Simmer (with lid on) for about 30 minutes, until rice is soft. Add more water if necessary, then stir in seasoning and parsley.

7. Cabbage and Hambone Soup   Serves 4

1 hambone
½ small cabbage (or
    about 8 oz (240 g)
    kale leaves—the
    coarser, older ones
    being quite suitable),
    shredded and
    chopped

1 oz (30 g) dripping
4 oz (120 g) onions,
    chopped
8 oz (240 g) potatoes,
    diced
pepper
¼ pt (1 ½ dl) milk

Melt dripping in a saucepan and fry onions gently for a few minutes. Add cabbage or kale leaves. Cook for about 5 minutes, stirring occasionally, then add hambone and potatoes. Cover with about 1 pt (6 dl) water. Simmer until all vegetables are tender (about 30 minutes), then remove and discard hambone. Rub the soup mixture through sieve, then return to saucepan and add seasoning and milk. Simmer for 1 minute.

8. Carrot and Oatmeal Soup (Cawl Moronen) Serves 4

8 oz (240 g) carrots,
    grated
1 oz (30 g) oatmeal
12 oz (360 g) onions,
    chopped small

1 oz (30 g) dripping
1 clove garlic, chopped
¼ pt (1 ½ dl) milk
salt, pepper
2 tbsps chopped parsley

Melt dripping in a saucepan and fry onions, carrots and garlic gently for 5 minutes. Cover with ¾ pt (4½ dl) water and simmer for 30 minutes. Mix oatmeal with milk, season and add to soup. Simmer (with lid on), stirring occasionally, until oatmeal is cooked (about 20 minutes), then stir in parsley.

9. Carrot and Onion Soup *Serves 4*

12 oz (360 g) carrots,
   chopped
8 oz (240 g) onions,
   chopped

pepper
½ tsp yeast extract
¼ pt (1 ½ dl) milk
2 tbsps chopped parsley

Simmer carrots and onions in ¾ pt (4 ½ dl) water in a saucepan until cooked (about 30 minutes). Stir in seasoning, yeast extract and milk. Bring to the boil, then stir in parsley.

10. Chestnut Soup *Serves 4*

4 oz (120 g) chestnuts,
   shelled and chopped
8 oz (240 g) potatoes,
   diced
3 oz (90 g) onions, sliced

1 oz (30 g) butter
¼ pt (1 ½ dl) milk
salt, pepper
2 tbsps chopped parsley

Simmer chestnuts, potatoes and onions in 1 pt (6 dl) water in a saucepan until all are tender (about 30 minutes). Mash, then stir in butter, milk and seasoning. Simmer for 5 minutes, then stir in parsley.

11. Jerusalem Artichoke Soup *Serves 4*

1 lb (480 g) Jerusalem
   artichokes, cut small
3 oz (90 g) onions,
   chopped
1 clove garlic, chopped

½ pt (3 dl) milk
½ oz (15 g) butter
salt, pepper
2 tbsps chopped parsley

Simmer Jerusalem artichokes, onions and garlic in 1 pt (6 dl) water in a saucepan until tender (about 30 minutes). Mash, add milk and bring to the boil, then stir in butter, seasoning and parsley.

12. Leaf and Bacon (Hungry Gap) Soup   Serves 4

2 rashers fat bacon, cut
    into small pieces
2 handfuls chickweed,
    chopped
2 handfuls young turnip
    tops, shredded and
    chopped
1 handful sorrel leaves,
    chopped

a few small cabbage or
    kale leaves, shredded
    and chopped
4 tbsps chopped chives
2 tbsps chopped fresh
    thyme
pepper
2 tbsps chopped parsley

Fry bacon in a saucepan (in own fat) until crisp. Add
1½ pts (9 dl) water and all other ingredients except
parsley. Bring to the boil and simmer for 45 minutes,
then stir in parsley.

13. Lettuce Cream Soup   Serves 4

This is a good way of using up lettuces that are bolting.

1 large lettuce (or
    equivalent amount of
    odd leaves),
    shredded and
    chopped
1 oz (30 g) butter
6 oz (180 g) onions,
    sliced

1 clove garlic, chopped
6 oz (180 g) turnips,
    grated
½ tsp grated nutmeg
1 tsp plain flour
¼ pt (1½ dl) milk
salt, pepper
2 tbsps chopped parsley

Melt butter in a saucepan and fry onions and garlic
gently for 5 minutes, then add lettuce and turnips.
Simmer gently (with lid on) for 30 minutes, turning
occasionally. Add ½ pt (3 dl) water and nutmeg, bring to
the boil and simmer for 10 minutes. Carefully mix flour
to a smooth paste with milk and add to soup. Bring to
the boil again, stirring continuously, season and
simmer for 5 minutes, then stir in parsley.

14. Lettuce and Weed Soup   *Serves 4*

This is another good way of using up lettuces that are bolting.

1 large lettuce (or
 equivalent amount of
 odd leaves),
 shredded and
 chopped
2 cups mixture of any of
 the following weed
 leaves: young nettles,
 sorrel, groundsel,
 chickweed, chopped

1 oz (30 g) butter
8 oz (240 g) onions,
 sliced
1 clove garlic, chopped
$\frac{1}{2}$ tsp yeast extract
pepper
2 tbsps chopped parsley

Melt butter in a saucepan and fry onions and garlic gently until tender. Press lettuce and mixed weeds into saucepan and cook gently (with lid on) for 10 minutes. Add $\frac{3}{4}$ pt (4$\frac{1}{2}$ dl) water and yeast extract. Bring to the boil, season and simmer for about 30 minutes, stirring occasionally, then stir in parsley.

15. Nettle and Vegetable Soup   *Serves 4*

sufficient young
 stinging nettle leaves
 and tops, chopped, to
 three-quarters fill a
 large saucepan
8 oz (240 g) mixed
 vegetables, chopped
 small

1 oz (30 g) butter
6 oz (180 g) onions,
 chopped
salt, pepper
$\frac{1}{4}$ pt (1$\frac{1}{2}$ dl) milk

Melt butter in a saucepan and fry onions until soft but not brown. Add vegetables, toss, then simmer gently (with lid on) for 5 minutes. Add nettles and simmer for 15 minutes. Add 1 pt (6 dl) water, season, bring to the boil and simmer until vegetables are tender. Stir in milk and re-heat.

16. Onion Soup   *Serves 4*

1 lb (480 g) onions,   salt, pepper
   chopped small $\frac{1}{2}$ pt (3 dl) milk
2 oz (60 g) butter   2 tbsps chopped parsley

Melt butter in a saucepan and fry onions gently until
golden-brown. Add seasoning and 1 pt (6 dl) water.
Bring to the boil and simmer for 45 minutes. Stir in milk
and re-heat, then stir in parsley.

17. Onion and Potato Soup   *Serves 4*

12 oz (360 g) onions,   1 clove garlic, chopped
   chopped small $\frac{1}{3}$ pt (2 dl) milk
8 oz (240 g) potatoes,   salt, pepper
   chopped   2 tbsps chopped parsley
1 oz (30 g) dripping

Melt dripping in a saucepan and fry onions and garlic
gently for a few minutes. Add potatoes and continue
cooking gently (with lid on) for about 10 minutes. Cover
with about $\frac{1}{2}$ pt (3 dl) water and simmer until onions are
tender and potatoes mushy. Stir in milk, bring to the
boil then stir in parsley.

18. Parsnip and Onion Soup   *Serves 4*

8 oz (240 g) parsnips,   1 tsp cornflour
   diced $\frac{1}{4}$ pt (1$\frac{1}{2}$ dl) milk
6 oz (180 g) onions,   salt, pepper
   sliced   2 tbsps chopped parsley
$\frac{1}{2}$ oz (15 g) butter

Melt butter in a saucepan and fry onions gently for a
few minutes. Add parsnip, toss around in pan, then
cook for 5 minutes (with lid on). Add 1 pt (6 dl) water
and simmer until parsnip is tender. Carefully mix cornflour to a smooth paste with milk and add to soup. Season, bring to the boil again, stirring continuously, and
simmer for 10 minutes. Then stir in parsley.

19. Pea Pod Soup

Serves 4

sufficient young pea
  pods to three-
  quarters fill a large
  saucepan
1 tsp sugar
6 oz (180 g) onions,
  chopped

1 clove garlic, chopped
$\frac{1}{2}$ tsp yeast extract
$\frac{1}{4}$ pt (1 $\frac{1}{2}$ dl) milk
2 tbsps chopped mint

Simmer pea pods with sugar in about 1$\frac{1}{2}$ pts (9 dl) water
in a saucepan for about 30 minutes. Strain and discard
pods. Add onions, garlic and yeast extract, then simmer until onions are tender. Stir in milk, simmer for 1
minute, then stir in mint.

20. Potato Cole (February) Soup

Serves 4

8 oz (240 g) potatoes,
  diced
8 oz (240 g) mixture of
  small cabbage hearts
  or leaves, shredded
  and chopped, and/or
  kale or sprouting
  broccoli shoots,

chopped, or old or
  'blown' Brussels
  sprouts, chopped
2 oz (60 g) dripping
a few small leeks or
  shallots, chopped
salt, pepper

Melt dripping in a saucepan and fry potatoes and leeks
(or shallots) gently until slightly brown. Add 1$\frac{1}{2}$ pts (9
dl) water, bring to the boil and simmer for 20 minutes.
Add 'greens', season, bring to the boil again and
simmer for 45 minutes.

21. Tomato and Onion Soup   *Serves 4*

This is a good recipe to use during a glut of tomatoes.

1 lb (480 g) ripe
   tomatoes, skinned
   and chopped
6 oz (180 g) onions,
   chopped small

$\frac{1}{2}$ oz (15 g) butter
cayenne pepper
salt
$\frac{1}{4}$ pt (1 $\frac{1}{2}$ dl) milk

Melt butter in a saucepan and fry onions gently for a few minutes, then add tomatoes, cayenne pepper, salt and 1 pt (6 dl) water. Bring to the boil and simmer for about 30 minutes. Mash, then stir in milk and re-heat.

22. Vegetable Marrow Soup   *Serves 4*

1 lb (480 g) marrow,
   diced
6 oz (180 g) tomatoes,
   sliced
6 oz (180 g) onions,
   sliced

1 oz (30 g) dripping
1 tsp Demerara sugar
1 tsp Worcestershire
   sauce
salt, pepper
2 tbsps chopped parsley

Simmer all ingredients, except parsley, in $\frac{1}{4}$ pt (1 $\frac{1}{2}$ dl) water in a saucepan (with lid on) for 1 $\frac{1}{2}$ hours, then stir in parsley.

23. Butter Bean and Tomato Soup   *Serves 4*

4 oz (120 g) butter
   beans, soaked
   overnight
8 oz (240 g) tomatoes,
   chopped (or 1 small
   can)

8 oz (240 g) onions,
   sliced
1 oz (30 g) butter
salt, pepper
2 tbsps chopped parsley

Simmer beans in 1 pt (6 dl) water in a saucepan until tender (about 2 hours). Fry onions gently in butter for a few minutes, then mix with butter beans. Add tomatoes, season, bring to the boil and simmer for about 15 minutes. Finally stir in parsley.

24. Haricot Bean and Tomato Soup   Serves 4

4 oz (120 g) haricot
   beans, soaked
   overnight
4 oz (120 g) tomatoes,
   chopped
4 oz (120 g) turnips, cut
   small
4 oz (120 g) onions,
   chopped

4 oz (120 g) potatoes,
   chopped
1 oz (30 g) dripping
1 dsp oatmeal
$\frac{1}{2}$ tsp cayenne pepper
salt
$\frac{1}{4}$ pt (1 $\frac{1}{2}$ dl) milk
2 tbsps chopped parsley

Simmer all ingredients, except milk and parsley, in
1 $\frac{1}{4}$ pt (7 $\frac{1}{2}$ dl) water in a saucepan (with lid on), until
beans are tender (about 2 hours). Stir in milk, simmer
for 1 minute, then stir in parsley.

25. Dried Pea Soup   Serves 4

4 oz (120 g) dried peas,
   soaked overnight
2 tbsps chopped fresh
   mint (or 1 tbsp dried
   mint)
5 oz (150 g) onions,
   sliced

4 oz (120 g) turnips,
   diced
2 oz (60 g) carrots, diced
1 clove garlic, chopped
1 dsp oatmeal
$\frac{1}{2}$ tsp yeast extract
pepper

Simmer peas and mint in 1 pt (6 dl) water in a saucepan
until tender (about 2 hours). Strain off liquor into a
bowl. Mash peas. Return liquor to pan and add all
other ingredients. Add water to cover, bring to the boil
and simmer for about 1 hour, stirring occasionally.

26. Dried Pea and Lettuce Soup
Serves 4

4 oz (120 g) dried peas,
  soaked overnight
1 large lettuce, chopped
4 oz (120 g) onions,
  grated
$\frac{1}{2}$ oz (15 g) butter

$\frac{1}{4}$ pt ($1\frac{1}{2}$ dl) milk
$\frac{1}{2}$ oz (15 g) plain flour
salt, pepper
1 oz (30 g) cheese,
  grated

Simmer peas in 1 pt (6 dl) water in a saucepan until tender (about 2 hours). Stir in lettuce and onion. Simmer for 30 minutes. Stir in butter and milk, then remove from heat. Blend flour and a little cold water to make a smooth paste and carefully mix with $\frac{1}{4}$ pt ($1\frac{1}{2}$ dl) of the soup, stirring continuously. Add thickening to bulk of soup, season, bring to the boil again and simmer for 5 minutes. Stir in cheese.

27. Lentil Soup
Serves 4

4 oz (120 g) lentils
1 oz (30 g) butter
8 oz (240 g) onions,
  sliced

1 clove garlic, chopped
pepper
$\frac{1}{2}$ tsp yeast extract
2 tbsps chopped parsley

Melt butter in a saucepan and fry onions and garlic gently for 10 minutes. Add lentils, mix thoroughly, and continue cooking for 5 minutes, stirring continuously. Add $1\frac{1}{2}$ pts (9 dl) water, seasoning and yeast extract and simmer until lentils are cooked and starting to break up (20 to 30 minutes), then stir in parsley.

28. Lentil and Vegetable Soup   *Serves 4*

4 oz (120 g) lentils
8 oz (240 g) mixed root
  and/or green vege-
  tables, chopped small
1 oz (30 g) dripping

8 oz (240 g) onions,
  chopped small
$\frac{1}{2}$ tsp yeast extract
$\frac{1}{2}$ tsp mixed dried herbs
pepper

Simmer lentils in $1\frac{1}{4}$ pts ($7\frac{1}{2}$ dl) water in a saucepan for 20 minutes. Melt dripping in another saucepan and fry onions gently for a few minutes. Add mixed vegetables and cook for 5 minutes, then add contents of first pan (add more water if necessary). Stir in yeast extract, herbs and seasoning, and simmer until all vegetables are tender (about 45 minutes).

29. Bread Soup (Cawl Bara Siloam)   *Serves 4*

2 oz (60 g) bread crusts,
  broken small
6 oz (180 g) onions,
  quartered
4 oz (120 g) turnips, cut
  small

$\frac{1}{2}$ pt (3 dl) milk
salt, pepper
$\frac{1}{2}$ oz (15 g) dripping
2 tbsps chopped chives
2 tbsps chopped parsley

Boil onions and turnips in $1\frac{1}{2}$ pts (9 dl) water for 20 minutes. Mash, then add bread. Simmer for 30 minutes, stirring occasionally (add water if necessary). Gradually add milk, stirring continuously. Bring to the boil and stir in seasoning, dripping, chives and parsley.

30. Bone Soup   Serves 4

8 oz – 1½ lb (240 – 720 g)
  fresh raw bones
1 dsp mixed dried herbs
12 oz (360 g) mixed root
  vegetables, diced
4 oz (120 g) onions,
  chopped

1 tbsp rice
½ tsp yeast extract
pepper
2 tbsps chopped parsley

Simmer bones and herbs in about 1½ pts (9 dl) water in
a saucepan for 2 hours. Remove and discard bones,
then add all other ingredients, except parsley. Simmer
again until rice is cooked and all vegetables are tender
(about 30 minutes), then stir in parsley.

31. Pig's Head Soup   Serves 4

½ pig's head, chopped in
  3 or 4 pieces to fit
  pan (each piece
  wrapped in muslin to
  contain bits of bone)
8 oz (240 g) mixed root
  vegetables, chopped
4 oz (120 g) onions,
  sliced
1 clove garlic, chopped

1 tsp mixed dried herbs
½ tsp mixed whole
  pickling spice (tied in
  muslin bag)
pepper
1 tsp yeast extract
1 tsp Worcestershire
  sauce
2 tbsps chopped parsley

Put all ingredients except seasoning, yeast extract,
Worcestershire sauce and parsley, into a large saucepan and simmer for 3 hours. Remove head pieces and
put aside for brawn (see recipe no. 75). Remove bag of
spices and discard. Strain off ½ pt (3 dl) of liquor from
soup and put aside for brawn. Stir seasoning, yeast
extract and Worcestershire sauce into soup and
simmer for 1 minute, then stir in parsley.

2. Meat Dishes

Meat dishes without pastry
32. Beef Stew
33. Beef and Bacon Savoury
34. Minced Beef Pie
35. Mincemeat Rissoles
36. Mincemeat Pancake
37. Cooked Meat Pudding
38. Cooked Meat Loaf
39. Cooked Meat Cakes
40. Corned Beef Hot Pot
41. Corned Beef Loaf
42. Lamb Stew
43. Stuffed Breast of Lamb
44. Lamb and Cheese Bake
45. Pork Stew
46. Stuffed Belly of Pork
47. Pork and Rice
48. Pork Pudding
49. Pork and Raisin Savoury
50. Pork and Egg Pancake
51. Ham and Egg Pie
52. Boiled Bacon and Rice
53. Bacon Hot Pot
54. Bacon and Onion in Batter
55. Bacon and Rice Mixture
56. Bacon and Swede
57. Sausage and Lentil Casserole
58. Sausage and Bacon Savoury
59. Sausage and Onion Pie
60. Sausage and Oatmeal Rissoles
61. Chicken Casserole
62. Chicken Leftovers and Rice
63. Rabbit Stew
64. Stuffed Rabbit
65. Rabbit and Tomatoes
66. Liver and Bacon Casserole
67. Liver, Bacon and Apple Casserole
68. Liver and Oatmeal Pudding
69. Liver and Onion Bake
70. Ox Heart and

Bacon Casserole
71. Kidney Casserole
72. Stuffed Lambs'
    Hearts
73. Sheep's Tongues
    Casserole
74. Sheep's Head Pie
75. Pig's Head Brawn
76. Faggots
77. Tripe and Onions
78. Tripe and Tomatoes

Meat dishes with pastry
79. Beef Roly-poly
80. Steak and Kidney
    Pudding
81. Thin Beef Pie
82. Beef and Vegetable
    Pie
83. Beef and Vegetable
    Pasties
84. Cooked Meat
    Pasties
85. Baked Pork Roll
86. Bacon Roly-poly
87. Bacon and Egg Pie
88. Bacon and Egg Flan
89. Bacon and Leek Pie
90. Bacon and Apple
    Pie
91. Bacon and Cheese
    Pasties
92. Sausage and Egg
    Pie
93. Rabbit Pie (1)
94. Rabbit Pie (2)
95. Liver and Bacon
    Roly-poly

MEAT DISHES WITHOUT PASTRY

In the lonely Welsh uplands there are still a few remote homesteads where a large pot hanging from a chain over an open fire is used for making a stew, or boiling meat dishes. Dilwen, our neighbour, lives in one such place, and the first time he called at Hafod and saw that we had replaced the kitchen fire with a solid fuel heat-retention cooker he was very disapproving. 'You can't cook Lob Scowse on that thing,' he muttered, 'It won't taste the same!'

We don't know why the unlikely term 'Lob Scowse' is used in the Welsh hills, nor are we sure how it is spelt, but the name is given to any form of meat and vegetable stew, and—Dilwen's disapproval notwithstanding — we have in fact cooked many pots of it in our Hafod stove. Recipe nos. 32, 42, 45 and 63 for stews are my versions of Lob Scowse, and the initial process of long,

43

very slow cooking of the meat is, I think, an important part. At Hafod I put my casserole in the bottom oven overnight, and it is this method I have quoted in the recipes, but now that I no longer own a solid fuel cooker I cook the meat overnight in a slow electric casserole.

I have suggested several other casserole dishes—all tasty and cheap—and also an assortment of ways in which sausages, liver and bacon can be cooked. But I have only two chicken recipes to offer. For one thing I consider that the best way to cook a chicken is to roast it with a good mixed herb stuffing, moreover, I will not buy a chicken unless I am reasonably sure that it has enjoyed a comparatively normal back-yard life. Such chickens are hard to come by these days—and they are expensive—so chicken doesn't appear very often on our table. When living at Hafod Alan occasionally 'earned' a small joint of lamb from a grateful farmer in return for a job done (receiving payment in the form of eggs or meat rather than cash was a much friendlier arrangement) but we were never given a chicken. Hens, it seems, were kept just to lay eggs; only a piece of roast lamb or a lamb stew was good enough for a man's dinner.

Dilwen always said that nothing was more comforting to him during a bitterly cold day out upon the hills than the knowledge that at home, in the warm kitchen, there was a pot full of meat and vegetables, or a liver and oatmeal pudding simmering away over the banked-up fire. But the pleasure of anticipating that delicious meal in the pot awaiting you at home is not one that is confined to cold men on lonely Welsh hills, and I have continued to dish up thick nourishing stews and tasty boiled puddings even though my Hafod cooker is now just a happy memory. We enjoy them as much now as we did then, but I must admit that the first time I prepared a stew in my new electric casserole Alan was extremely doubtful. 'You can't cook Lob Scowse in that thing,' he muttered, 'It won't taste the same!'

32. Beef Stew

Serves 4 – 6

1 ½ lb (720 g) shin of
  beef, cubed
1 clove garlic, chopped
1 dsp mixed dried herbs
1 ½ lb (720 g) mixed root
  vegetables, diced
12 oz (360 g) onions,
  sliced

4 oz (120 g) lentils
1 tbsp pearl barley
1 tsp yeast extract
pepper
2 tbsps plain flour

Put meat, garlic and herbs in a casserole. Well cover
with water, put lid on, bring to the boil and then cook
overnight in a very slow oven. Next day add all other
ingredients, except flour. Add more water to well
cover; bring to the boil then cook in casserole with lid
on in a slow oven for about 4 hours. Make a thin paste
of flour and a little cold water and gradually stir into
stew. Increase heat to allow stew to boil and thicken.

33. Beef and Bacon Savoury

Serves 4

8 oz (240 g) minced beef
8 oz (240 g) streaky
  bacon, cut small
10 oz (300 g) onions,
  chopped
dripping for frying

1 ½ lb (720 g) boiled
  potatoes, mashed
2 tsps mixed dried
  herbs
salt, pepper

Fry beef, bacon and onions gently in dripping until
cooked (turning frequently). Mix with all other ingredients, then turn into a well-greased pie dish and bake
in a hot oven until brown (about 30 minutes).

34. Minced Beef Pie (Pastai Bugail)   Serves 4

12 oz (360 g) minced
    beef
1 oz (30 g) dripping
6 oz (180 g) parsnips,
    grated
8 oz (240 g) carrots,
    grated
6 oz (180 g) onions,
    sliced
2 tsps mixed dried
    herbs

pepper
1 tsp yeast extract
    dissolved in $\frac{1}{4}$ pt
    (1 $\frac{1}{2}$ dl) hot water
1 $\frac{1}{2}$ lb (720 g) potatoes
a little butter
a little milk
grated nutmeg
2 oz (60 g) rolled oats

Melt dripping in a saucepan and rapidly brown minced beef, turning frequently, for 5 minutes. Add all vegetables (except potatoes), herbs and pepper. Mix well together and cook gently (with lid on), over a low heat for 10 minutes. Add the yeast extract stock, put lid on again and simmer for 45 minutes, stirring occasionally. Meanwhile boil potatoes and mash with butter, milk and a sprinkle of nutmeg. Add the rolled oats to the vegetable and meat mixture and continue cooking until all liquor is absorbed. Turn into a greased pie dish, cover with potatoes and smooth top firmly. Bake in a hot oven until crisp and brown on top (20 to 30 minutes).

35. Mincemeat Rissoles   Makes 10–12

8 oz (240 g) minced beef
3 oz (90 g) onions,
    grated
2 oz (60 g) breadcrumbs

1 tsp mixed dried herbs
salt, pepper
a little plain flour
fat for frying

Mix together all ingredients except flour and fat, then with well-floured hands form into little flat cakes and fry each side gently until brown (about 15 minutes).

36. Mincemeat Pancake   *Serves 2*

8 oz (240 g) minced beef
3 oz (90 g) onions,
   minced
1 egg, beaten
2 oz (60 g) breadcrumbs

1 oz (30 g) raisins,
   minced
salt, pepper
a little plain flour
fat for frying

Mix all ingredients except flour and fat, then with well-floured hands form into cake to fit an 8-in (20-cm) pan.
Fry gently for about 25 minutes, then divide in two and carefully turn each half over, adding fat if necessary.
Continue cooking for about 20 minutes.

37. Cooked Meat Pudding (Pwdin Gelli)   *Serves 4*

1 lb (480 g) cooked meat,
   minced
4 oz (120 g)
   breadcrumbs
$\frac{1}{2}$ pt (3 dl) milk
8 oz (240 g) boiled
   potatoes, mashed

4 oz (120 g) onion,
   grated
1 tsp rosemary,
   chopped
salt, pepper
a little lard or dripping
a little oatmeal

Soak breadcrumbs in milk for 30 minutes. Beat well, then add all other ingredients except lard and oatmeal.
Mix well. Turn mixture into a pie dish well greased with lard and coated with oatmeal. Bake in a moderate oven for 45 minutes.

38. Cooked Meat Loaf

Serves 4

12 oz (360 g) leftover
   meat, minced
1 oz (30 g) dripping
1 oz (30 g) plain flour
5 oz (150 g) onions,
   grated

$\frac{1}{2}$ tsp yeast extract
1 tsp Worcestershire
   sauce
pepper
1 egg, separated

Melt dripping in a saucepan, stir in flour. Remove from heat and slowly stir in $\frac{1}{4}$ pt ($1\frac{1}{2}$ dl) water. Return to heat and cook slowly until mixture thickens. Stir in all other ingredients except egg white. Whisk egg white stiff and fold into mixture. Pour into a well-greased pie dish and bake in a moderate oven until browned (about 25 minutes).

39. Cooked Meat Cakes

Makes 8 – 10

6 – 8 oz (180 – 240 g)
   leftover meat,
   minced
3 oz (90 g) onions,
   grated
2 oz (60 g) self-raising
   flour

1 oz (30 g) suet
2 tbsps chopped parsley
1 tsp mixed dried herbs
$\frac{1}{2}$ tsp curry powder
salt

Make a stiff mixture of all ingredients with 2 or 3 tbsps water and fill well-greased patty tins. Bake in a moderately hot oven until crisp and brown (about 15 minutes).

40. Corned Beef Hot Pot   Serves 4

1 12-oz (360-g) can
  corned beef, chopped
6 oz (180 g) tomatoes,
  sliced (or 1 small can)
6 oz (180 g) onions,
  chopped
6 oz (180 g) carrots,
  grated
4 tbsps chopped parsley

2 tsps mixed dried
  herbs
a little Worcestershire
  sauce
salt, pepper
1½ lb (720 g) potatoes,
  sliced
a little dripping

Mix all ingredients together except potatoes and dripping. (Add 2 or 3 tbsps water if using fresh tomatoes.)
Turn mixture into a well-greased casserole; cover with
potatoes and dot with dripping. Put lid on and cook in a
moderately hot oven for 45 minutes. Remove lid and
continue cooking for 1 hour.

41. Corned Beef Loaf   Serves 4

1 12-oz (360-g) can
  corned beef, chopped
1 tsp yeast extract
  dissolved in 4 tbsps
  hot water
1½ lb (720 g) boiled
  potatoes, mashed
6 oz (180 g) onions,
  grated

2 oz (60 g) breadcrumbs
4 tbsps chopped parsley
1 tsp mixed dried herbs
a little Worcestershire
  sauce
pepper

Mix all ingredients together and turn into a well-
greased 2-lb (or 1-kg) loaf tin. Cover with foil and bake
in a moderate oven for 45 minutes. Remove foil and
continue cooking for 15 minutes.

42. Lamb Stew

Serves 4–6

2 lb (960 g) neck of lamb, cut small (or large breast of lamb cut small)

1 large sprig of rosemary

1½ lb (720 g) root vegetables, diced

12 oz (360 g) onions, sliced

8 oz (240 g) tomatoes, sliced

2 tbsps dried peas, soaked overnight

1 tbsp pearl barley

1 tsp yeast extract

1 tbsp dried herbs

2 tbsps dried mint

2 tbsps plain flour

4 tbsps chopped parsley

Put meat and rosemary in a casserole. Well cover with water, put lid on, bring to the boil, then cook overnight in a very slow oven. Remove and discard rosemary and bones next day, and add all other ingredients except flour and parsley. Add more water to well cover; bring to the boil, then cook in casserole (with lid on) in a slow oven for about 4 hours. Make a thin paste of flour and a little cold water and gradually stir into stew. Increase heat to allow stew to boil and thicken. Stir in parsley.

43. Stuffed Breast of Lamb

Serves 4

1 large breast of lamb with bones removed (see recipe no. 30, Bone Soup)

mixed herb stuffing or mint stuffing (see recipes nos. 303 and 304)

Cover lamb with stuffing, roll up and secure with skewer or string. Place in a baking tin, cover with lid or foil and roast in a hot oven for 10 minutes, then in a slow oven for 2 hours.

44. Lamb and Cheese Bake

Serves 4

8 oz (240 g) cooked
  lamb, minced
4 oz (120 g) cheese,
  grated
8 oz (240 g) tomatoes,
  chopped
white sauce (as recipe
  no. 305), using
  1oz (30 g) butter,

1 oz (30 g) flour and
  $\frac{1}{4}$ pt (1 $\frac{1}{2}$ dl) milk
6 oz (180 g) onions,
  grated
1 tsp mixed dried herbs
1 level tsp dry mustard
salt, pepper
1 $\frac{1}{2}$ lb (720 g) boiled
  potatoes, sliced

Mix together all ingredients except the potatoes and
half the cheese. Turn into a greased pie dish, cover
with potatoes and sprinkle rest of cheese over. Bake
in a moderate oven until golden-brown (about 45
minutes).

45. Pork Stew

Serves 4–6

2 lb (960 g) belly pork,
  cut small
1 clove garlic, chopped
1 dsp mixed dried herbs
1 $\frac{1}{2}$ lb (720 g) root
  vegetables, diced
12 oz (360 g) onions,
  sliced

2 tbsps haricot beans
1 tbsp pearl barley
1 tsp yeast extract
1 dsp Worcestershire
  sauce
pepper
2 tbsps plain flour
4 tbsps chopped parsley

Put meat, garlic and herbs in a casserole. Well cover
with water, put lid on, bring to the boil, then cook overnight in a very slow oven. Next day add all other ingredients except flour and parsley. Add more water to
well cover; bring to the boil, then cook in casserole
(with lid on) in a slow oven for about 4 hours. Make a
thin paste of flour and a little cold water and gradually
stir into stew. Increase heat to allow stew to boil and
thicken. Stir in parsley.

46. Stuffed Belly of Pork   Serves 4

2 lb (960 g) belly pork   mixed herb stuffing (see
                                 recipe no. 303)

Slice pork almost in two (so that the top half—with
'crackling'—is hinged on one side.) Spread stuffing
inside, fold over and secure with skewer or string.
Place in a baking tin, cover with lid or foil and bake in a
hot oven for 15 minutes, then in a slow oven for 2 hours.

47. Pork and Rice   Serves 4

12 oz (360 g) belly pork   3 oz (90 g) cooking
  (with rind removed),   apples, chopped
  cut small   1 clove garlic, chopped
6 oz (180 g) rice   1 tsp mixed dried herbs
$\frac{1}{2}$ oz (15 g) dripping   pepper
8 oz (240 g) carrots, $\frac{1}{2}$ tsp yeast extract
  chopped   dissolved in $\frac{3}{4}$ pt
4 oz (120 g) onions,   (4 $\frac{1}{2}$ dl) hot water
  chopped
4 oz (120 g) tomatoes,
  chopped

Melt dripping in a saucepan and fry pork gently for 15
minutes. Add all other ingredients except rice and
yeast extract stock. Toss around and continue cooking
in a closed pan for 5 minutes. Add yeast extract stock
and simmer for 15 minutes. Add rice (and more water if
necessary). Continue simmering until rice is cooked
and most of the liquor absorbed (about 20 minutes).

48. Pork Pudding   Serves 4

1 lb (480 g) pork   2 tbsps chopped parsley
   sausage meat   1 tsp mixed dried herbs
4 oz (120 g) streaky   1 dsp chutney (or fruit
   bacon, cut small   sauce)
1 egg, beaten   1 tsp dry mustard
2 oz (60 g) breadcrumbs

Fry bacon gently. Add sausage meat and fork around
until partly cooked. Mix thoroughly with all other
ingredients. Turn into a 2-pt (12-dl) greased pudding
basin and boil for $2\frac{1}{2}$ hours.

49. Pork and Raisin Savoury   Serves 4

12 oz (360 g) cooked $\frac{1}{3}$ pt (2 dl) milk
   belly pork, cut small   8 oz (240 g) self-raising
3 oz (90 g) raisins (or   flour
   chopped dates or   salt, pepper
   grated apple) $\frac{1}{2}$ oz (15 g) pork dripping
1 egg

Beat egg in milk, then gradually beat in flour. Add all
other ingredients, except dripping, and mix well. Turn
into a baking tin well greased with the dripping and
cook in a moderate oven for 45 minutes.

50. Pork and Egg Pancake (Crempog Cig Moch)

Serves 2

6 oz (180 g) slice of belly
   pork (rind removed),
   cut small
8 oz (240 g) potatoes,
   diced

3 eggs
salt, pepper
2 tbsps chopped parsley
fat for frying

Fry pork gently in own fat for 15 minutes. Add potatoes and continue frying until mixture is cooked, turning frequently and adding fat as necessary. Beat eggs with seasoning and parsley and pour over pork mixture. Increase heat and cook until almost set. Divide in two and carefully turn each half over. Continue cooking for 2 minutes.

51. Ham and Egg Pie

Serves 4

8 oz (240 g) cooked ham
   (or boiled bacon),
   chopped
3 eggs, beaten
4 tbsps chopped parsley

salt, pepper
$\frac{1}{4}$ pt ($1\frac{1}{2}$ dl) milk
1 oz (30 g) butter
4 oz (120 g)
   breadcrumbs

Mix all ingredients together except butter and half the breadcrumbs. Put into a greased pie dish and top with rest of breadcrumbs. Dot with butter and bake in a moderately hot oven for 30 minutes.

52. Boiled Bacon and Rice   *Serves 4*

8 oz (240 g) boiled
  bacon, chopped
6 oz (180 g) rice
2 oz (60 g) dripping
8 oz (240 g) onions,
  sliced
2 oz (60 g) nuts, chopped
6 oz (180 g) tomatoes,
  sliced

2 oz (60 g) sultanas
1 tsp yeast extract
  dissolved in 1 $\frac{1}{2}$ pts
  (9 dl) hot water
pepper
4 tbsps chopped parsley

Melt dripping in a saucepan and fry onions gently until cooked but not brown. Add rice and nuts and continue cooking for 10 minutes (stirring continuously). Add all other ingredients except parsley. Put lid on, bring to the boil and simmer until rice is cooked and most liquid absorbed (about 20 minutes), then stir in parsley.

53. Bacon Hot Pot (Pwdin Cig Moch)   *Serves 4*

1 lb (480 g) streaky
  bacon
8 oz (240 g) onions,
  sliced
6 oz (180 g) carrots,
  sliced
4 tbsps chopped parsley

pepper
1 $\frac{1}{2}$ lb (720 g) potatoes,
  sliced
$\frac{1}{2}$ tsp yeast extract
  dissolved in $\frac{1}{4}$ pt
  (1 $\frac{1}{2}$ dl) hot water

Fry bacon gently in own fat for 5 minutes, then mix with all other ingredients except 4 oz (120 g) of potatoes and yeast extract stock. Turn into a greased pie dish, top with rest of potatoes and pour yeast extract stock over. Cover with foil and cook in a hot oven for 10 minutes, then in a slow oven for 2 hours. Remove foil and continue to cook until potato is brown (about 30 minutes).

54. Bacon and Onion in Batter

Serves 4

1 lb (480 g) streaky
  bacon, cut small
1 lb (480 g) onions,
  sliced

3 tbsps self-raising flour
2 eggs, beaten
$\frac{1}{2}$ pt (3 dl) milk
pepper

Fry bacon gently in own fat. Add onions and fry until soft but not brown. Make batter by gently stirring flour into eggs then slowly beating in milk. Add pepper and beat well. Put bacon and onions in a well-greased pie dish, pour batter over and bake in a moderately hot oven for 30 minutes.

55. Bacon and Rice Mixture (Children's Mixture)

Serves 4

12 oz (360 g) streaky
  bacon, cut small
6 oz (180 g) boiled rice
2 oz (60 g) dripping
12 oz (360 g) boiled
  potatoes, chopped

3 hardboiled eggs,
  chopped
4 tbsps chopped parsley
pepper

Fry bacon in dripping until slightly crisp. Remove from pan, then fry potatoes until slightly browned. Mix all ingredients together, turn into a greased baking tin and cook in a hot oven for 15 to 20 minutes.

56. Bacon and Swede (Stwnch Cig Moch)

Serves 2 – 4

8 oz (240 g) streaky
  bacon (preferably
  smoked)

1 lb (480 g) swedes,
  sliced thin
pepper

Place a few rashers of bacon in a saucepan. Cover with a layer of swedes and sprinkle pepper over. Repeat layers, finishing with a sprinkle of pepper. Add a few tablespoons of water and put lid on. Bring slowly to the boil and then simmer very gently for 1 hour.

57. Sausage and Lentil Casserole   *Serves 4*

1 lb (480 g) pork
  sausages
4 oz (120 g) lentils
2 oz (60 g) dripping
12 oz (360 g) onions,
  sliced

1 clove garlic, chopped
1 tsp yeast extract
  dissolved in 1 pint
  (6 dl) hot water
pepper

Melt dripping in pan and fry onions gently until cooked but not brown, then place in a well-greased casserole. Prick and brown sausages quickly in a very hot pan, then place them on the onions and pour fat over. Add all other ingredients, put lid on and cook in hot oven for 10 minutes, then in a slow oven for 2 hours.

58. Sausage and Bacon Savoury   *Serves 4*

1 lb (480 g) pork
  sausage meat
6 oz (180 g) streaky
  bacon, cut small
6 oz (180 g)
  breadcrumbs
4 tbsps chopped parsley

2 tbsps tomato sauce
$\frac{1}{2}$ tsp yeast extract
  dissolved in 2 tbsps
  hot water
pepper
a little dripping

Fry bacon gently in own fat. When fat is running freely fork in sausage meat and cook gently for 15 minutes (turning frequently). Remove from heat and mix in all other ingredients except dripping. Turn into a well-greased pie dish, dot with dripping and bake in a moderately hot oven for 30 minutes.

59. Sausage and Onion Pie   *Serves 4*

1 lb (480 g) sausage
    meat
8 oz (240 g) onions,
    chopped
1 oz (30 g) dripping
8 tbsps chopped parsley
1 tsp dried sage

a little Worcestershire
    sauce
1 ½ lb (720 g) boiled
    potatoes, mashed
    with butter, milk and
    a little grated nutmeg

Melt dripping in a saucepan and fry sausage meat and onions together gently for 20 minutes, turning frequently. Remove from heat and mix with all other ingredients except potatoes. Put half the potatoes into a greased pie dish and fork down smoothly. Turn sausage mixture on to this, then cover with remaining potato. Smooth top firmly then bake in a hot oven until crisp and brown on top (20 to 30 minutes).

60. Sausage and Oatmeal Rissoles   *Makes 10 – 12*

6 oz (180 g) pork
    sausage meat,
    chopped small
4 oz (120 g) oatmeal
4 oz (120 g) onions,
    grated

1 tsp mixed dried herbs
salt, pepper
a little plain flour
fat for frying

Simmer oatmeal in ½ pt (3 dl) slightly salted water, stirring continuously. When thick, stir in all other ingredients except flour and fat. Leave to cool, then with floured hands form into little flat cakes, cover with flour, then fry each side gently until brown (about ten minutes).

61. Chicken Casserole   *Serves 4*

4 chicken joints
4 oz (120 g) butter
1 lb (480 g) shallots (or
   small onions), peeled
   and left whole
2 tbsps plain flour

$\frac{3}{4}$ pt ($4\frac{1}{2}$ dl) milk
salt, pepper
1 tbsp chopped parsley
1 tbsp chopped chives
2 tsps mixed dried
   herbs

Melt butter in a frying pan and fry joints for a few minutes, turning to brown each side. Put joints in casserole. Meanwhile put shallots in saucepan, cover with water, bring to the boil and simmer for 5 minutes. Then drain and add to chicken. Stir flour into the hot fat in frying pan and gradually blend in milk to make smooth sauce. Cook gently for a few minutes, then add all other ingredients. Pour sauce over chicken and shallots. Put lid on and cook in a moderate oven for 1 hour.

62. Chicken Leftovers and Rice   *Serves 4*

bits picked from
   chicken carcass and
   stuffing (about 4
   cupfuls)
6 oz (180 g) rice
1 oz (30 g) chicken
   dripping (plus any
   jelly)

6 oz (180 g) onions,
   sliced
8 oz (240 g) tomatoes,
   chopped
6 oz (180 g) cooking
   apples, chopped
2 oz (60 g) raisins
salt, pepper

Melt dripping in a saucepan and fry onions gently for 5 minutes. Add rice and fry for a few minutes, stirring continuously. Add $\frac{3}{4}$ pt ($4\frac{1}{2}$ dl) water and then all other ingredients. Put lid on, bring to the boil and simmer until rice is cooked and has absorbed most of the liquor (about 20 minutes).

63. Rabbit Stew
Serves 4–6

1 medium rabbit,
  jointed
1 dsp mixed dried herbs
$1\frac{1}{2}$ lb (720 g) mixed root
  vegetables, diced
8 oz (240 g) tomatoes,
  sliced

8 oz (240 g) onions,
  sliced
1 tbsp pearl barley
1 tsp yeast extract
1 tsp curry powder
pepper
2 tbsps plain flour

Put rabbit and herbs in a casserole. Well cover with water, put lid on, bring to the boil, then cook overnight in a very slow oven. Next day remove and discard bones and add all other ingredients, except flour. Add more water to well cover; bring to the boil, then cook in casserole with lid on in a slow oven for about 4 hours. Make a thin paste of flour and a little cold water and gradually stir into stew. Increase heat to allow stew to boil and thicken.

64. Stuffed Rabbit
Serves 4

1 medium rabbit,
  dressed
mixed herb stuffing (see
  recipe no. 303)

4 oz (120 g) streaky
  bacon

Stuff rabbit and tie in two places with string. Put into a baking tin with about 1 in ($2\frac{1}{2}$ cm) water. Place bacon on top and cover with lid or foil. Bake in a hot oven for 15 minutes, then in a moderate oven for 30 minutes. Remove lid or foil and continue cooking in a moderate oven for a further 30 minutes, basting occasionally.

65. Rabbit and Tomatoes   Serves 4

4 joints of rabbit
1 small tin tomatoes
2 oz (60 g) dripping
4 rashers streaky
    bacon, cut small
8 oz (240 g) onions,
    sliced

1 tsp yeast extract
dash of Worcestershire
    sauce
pepper
4 tbsps chopped parsley

Melt dripping in a saucepan and fry rabbit, bacon and onions for 5 minutes, turning frequently. Cover with water, put lid on, bring to the boil and simmer until meat is tender ($1 - 1\frac{1}{2}$ hours). Lift joints from pan and remove and discard bones. Return to pan with tomatoes, yeast extract, Worcestershire sauce and seasoning. Bring to the boil, then add parsley.

66. Liver and Bacon Casserole   Serves 4

8 oz (240 g) pig's liver,
    sliced
6 oz (180 g) streaky
    bacon, cut small
1 oz (30 g) dripping
8 oz (240 g) onions,
    sliced

6 oz (180 g) tomatoes,
    sliced (or 1 small can)
pepper
2 oz (60 g) plain flour
$\frac{1}{2}$ tsp yeast extract
    dissolved in $\frac{3}{4}$ pt
    ($4\frac{1}{2}$ dl) hot water

Fry liver and bacon gently in dripping for 10 minutes. Remove from pan and put into a casserole. Fry onions (and tomatoes if using fresh ones) until soft then put them on top of the liver and bacon. Add seasoning. Make a sauce by carefully stirring flour into the bacon fat and adding yeast extract stock (or tomato juice if using canned tomatoes—which should be put into casserole at this stage). Pour sauce into casserole, put lid on and cook in a moderate oven for $1\frac{1}{2}$ hours.

67. Liver, Bacon and Apple Casserole   Serves 4

8 oz (240 g) pig's liver,
    cut small
6 oz (180 g) streaky
    bacon, cut small
8 oz (240 g) cooking
    apples, grated
1 oz (30 g) dripping
8 oz (240 g) onions,
    grated

4 tbsps chopped parsley
1 tsp mixed dried herbs
pepper
1 tsp yeast extract
    dissolved in $\frac{1}{4}$ pt
    $(1\frac{1}{2}$ dl) hot water
4 oz (120 g)
    breadcrumbs

Fry liver and bacon gently in dripping for 10 minutes.
Turn into a bowl with all other ingredients except
yeast extract and breadcrumbs. Mix well, then put
into a casserole. Add yeast extract stock. Top up with
sufficient water to almost cover. Sprinkle breadcrumbs over, put lid on and cook in a moderately hot
oven for 1 hour. Remove lid and cook for a further 15
minutes.

68. Liver and Oatmeal Pudding   Serves 4

5 oz (150 g) pig's liver
8 oz (240 g) oatmeal
1 oz (30 g) pearl barley
4 oz (120 g) onions,
    grated

2 oz (60 g) dripping
1 tsp mixed dried herbs
1 tsp yeast extract
$\frac{1}{2}$ tsp dry mustard
salt, pepper

Soak oatmeal in $\frac{1}{2}$ pt (3 dl) water. Meanwhile simmer
liver and barley in 1 pt (6 dl) water in a saucepan (with
lid on) for 1 hour. Remove from heat. Take out liver and
cut into small pieces. Return to pan with all other
ingredients. Stir thoroughly, then turn into well-
greased 2-pt (12-dl) pudding basin and boil for 2 hours.

Any leftovers may be sliced, floured and fried on
both sides.

69. Liver and Onion Bake   Serves 4

1 lb (480 g) pig's liver,
   sliced
10 oz (300 g) onions,
   chopped
fat for frying
2 dsps plain flour

1 tsp yeast extract
1½ lb (720 g) boiled
   potatoes, mashed
2 tsps mixed dried
   herbs
salt, pepper

Fry liver and onions gently until cooked but not brown.
Remove from pan and cut liver into small pieces. Put
flour and yeast extract into the pan and mix smoothly
with the fat, then slowly stir in 4 tbsps water to make a
gravy. Mix gravy with all other ingredients, then turn
into a well-greased meat tin. Fork top smooth and bake
in a hot oven until brown (about 30 minutes).

70. Ox Heart and Bacon Casserole   Serves 4

8 oz (240 g) ox heart,
   very thinly sliced
6 oz (80 g) streaky
   bacon, cut small
1½ lb (720 g) potatoes,
   sliced
12 oz (360 g) onions,
   sliced

2 tsps mixed dried
   herbs
pepper
1 tsp yeast extract
   dissolved in ½ pt (3 dl)
   hot water

Put layers of potatoes, heart, bacon and onions into a
casserole. Sprinkle with herbs and pepper. Repeat
layers, finishing with potatoes. Pour over yeast extract
stock. Put lid on and cook in a moderately hot oven for 3
hours. Remove lid and cook for a further 15 minutes.

71. Kidney Casserole

Serves 4

7 or 8 lambs' kidneys,
sliced (or 3 pigs'
kidneys, sliced)
8 oz (240 g) onions,
sliced

2 tsps mixed dried
herbs
pepper
1 tbsp plain flour
$\frac{1}{2}$ tsp yeast extract

Put alternate layers of kidney and onions sprinkled
with herbs and seasoning into a casserole. Half fill
with water and put lid on. Cook in a hot oven for 15
minutes, then in a slow oven for 1 hour. Make paste
with flour, yeast extract and water; thin down with
liquor from casserole. Stir into casserole and cook for
a further 10 minutes.

72. Stuffed Lambs' Hearts

Serves 4

4 prepared lambs'
hearts, cut open
mixed herb stuffing (see
recipe no. 303)

4 oz (120 g) streaky
bacon
a little dripping

Put hearts in a casserole, cover with water and cook in
a slow oven overnight. Divide stuffing into four and
wrap each heart around a ball of stuffing. Pack hearts
(cut-side down) in baking tin well greased with dripping. Lay rashers of bacon over them. Cover with lid or
foil and bake in a moderate oven for 1 hour.

73. Sheep's Tongues Casserole   Serves 4

4 sheep's tongues,
  soaked overnight in
  salt water
1 clove garlic, chopped
4 oz (120 g) streaky
  bacon
1½ lb (720 g) mixed root
  vegetables, diced

6 oz (180 g) onions,
  sliced
1 tsp mixed dried herbs
1 tsp yeast extract
pepper

Wash tongues well, then simmer with garlic in 1 pt
(6 dl) water in a saucepan for 2½ hours. Drain and keep
liquor. Skin and chop tongues. Place half the bacon in a
casserole and cover with mixture of tongues and all
other ingredients, including yeast extract dissolved in
liquor. Place remaining bacon on top, put lid on and
cook in moderate oven for 2 hours.

74. Sheep's Head Pie   Serves 4

1 sheep's head, split in
  two, and soaked
  overnight in salt
  water
8 oz (240 g) onions,
  quartered
1 tbsp chopped
  rosemary

1 tsp yeast extract
4 oz (120 g) rice
4 oz (120 g)
  breadcrumbs
2 tbsps chopped parsley
pepper
8 oz (240 g) tomatoes,
  sliced

Drain and well wash head, removing all loose bits of
bone, then simmer in a saucepan with onion, rosemary
and yeast extract for 1½ hours. Add rice and simmer
for 30 minutes. Remove head and pick off all bits of
meat. Return meat to pan, then strain off liquor into a
jug. Mix breadcrumbs, parsley and pepper and place a
layer in a well-greased pie dish. Mix tomatoes with all
other ingredients and put a layer into the pie dish.
Repeat layers, finishing with breadcrumb mixture.
Pour ¼ pt (1½ dl) of sheep's head liquor over, and cook in
a hot oven for 30 minutes. (The remaining liquor can be
added to soup or stew, or used to make gravy.)

75. Pig's Head Brawn   *Makes about a 2-lb (or 1-kg)*
basin full

half pig's head, saved $\frac{1}{2}$ *pt (3 dl) liquor, saved*
   from soup (see recipe   *from soup*
   no. 31)

Skim fat from liquor (which will have jelled if cold) and put aside for use as dripping. Pick all meat from bones and cut small. Add to liquor and boil for a few minutes, then pour into basin. Allow to set in cool place overnight.

To obtain further dripping, render down all fatty bits remaining on head pieces.

Brawn can also be made from any scraps of cooked meat simmered for a few minutes with the strained liquor from boiled pigs' trotters. Pigs' trotters have little or no meat on them, but as they are available for a few pence (I know a butcher who gives them away) they are well worth having.

76. Faggots   *Serves 4*

$1\frac{1}{2}$ *lb (720 g) pig's fry*   *1 piece of caul*
   (heart, liver, lights,   *1 dsp mixed dried herbs*
   etc.)   *salt, pepper*
6 oz (180 g) onions   *a little dripping*
3 oz (90 g) bread

Mince pig's fry, onions and bread. Mix well with herbs and seasoning. Put 2 tbsps of mixture on to roughly 4 in (10 cm) squares of caul. Roll over to form balls, then pack closely in a baking tin well greased with dripping (with edges of caul underneath). Cover with lid or foil and bake in a moderate oven for 1 hour.

77. Tripe and Onions   Serves 4

1 lb (480 g) tripe, cut
   small
12 oz (360 g) onions,
   sliced
½ pt (3 dl) milk

2 oz (60 g) butter
2 dsps plain flour
salt, pepper
4 tbsps chopped parsley

Simmer tripe and onion in milk with ½ pt (3 dl) water in
a saucepan for 45 minutes. Cream butter with flour
and seasoning and add water to make a paste, then stir
slowly into tripe and onion. Put lid on, bring to the boil
and simmer for 30 minutes, then stir in parsley.

78. Tripe and Tomatoes   Serves 4

1 lb (480 g) tripe, cut
   small
8 oz (240 g) tomatoes,
   chopped
2 oz (60 g) dripping
6 oz (180 g) onions,
   sliced

2 tbsps plain flour
½ pt (3 dl) milk
1 tsp mixed dried herbs
salt, pepper
4 tbsps chopped parsley

Melt dripping in a saucepan and fry onion gently until
slightly browned. Remove from heat and stir in flour.
Add milk and ½ pt (3 dl) water, then stir in tripe and all
other ingredients except parsley. Put lid on, bring to
the boil and simmer for 1¼ hours, then stir in parsley.

MEAT DISHES WITH PASTRY

There is something mysterious about pastry. You and I
could follow identical recipes—yet the pastry produced would be quite different. My mother made
melt-in-the-mouth short-crust pastry; so did my mother-
in-law. My father can produce an excellent pie crust
too. All of them good—but all different.

Alan has never been particularly enthusiastic about

my pastry. He eats it without comment. So he was amazed at the glowing praises it received when we were in service together. As a professional cook (albeit always a humble temporary stand-in) my concoctions were wholesome and nourishing if not exotic and exciting, and my pastry was always ecstatically received. In fact one lady insisted that I spent my last week with her knocking-up bowl after bowl of pastry for her to put in the deep freeze. She was determined that her pies and puddings for many months after our departure would still be wrapped in my pastry. (Alan claims that this was just another example of her very suspect gastronomic standards. As this lady ate chocolate and soup for breakfast and liked chip sandwiches for her supper perhaps he is right.)

However, qualities of pastry notwithstanding, any cook who wants to make a small amount of meat stretch a bit further will find that there is no method more successful than enfolding it in pastry. A beef and vegetable pie of golden short-crust (crisp on top but moist and soft on the inside where it absorbs the gravy), or a boiled meat pudding, succulent with herbs and onion, will satisfy the hungriest and most demanding of meat-eaters. And for the person who is away from home all day and wants to carry something nourishing and sustaining, there is nothing to beat a nice fat pasty. I always make my pasties large—in the true Cornish tradition. (The tin-miner's wife, I have read, always ensured that her man took with him a solid meal of meat and vegetables wrapped in pastry.) And in spite of Alan's contention that probably the best place to eat my pastry is several miles underground in the dark, I find that the pasties, pies and puddings in this household disappear as fast as I can make them.

79. Beef Roly-poly

Serves 4

1 lb (480 g) minced
   beef
8 oz (240 g) onions,
   grated
2 tsps mixed dried
   herbs
salt, pepper

1 oz (30 g) dripping
suet pastry (as recipe
   no. 297), using 4 oz
   (120 g) suet and 8 oz
   (240 g) self-raising
   flour

Mix together all ingredients except dripping and
pastry and gently fry in dripping for 15 minutes (stirring continuously). Roll out pastry into oblong and
moisten edges. Spread mixture over, then roll up
and seal edges. Tie in cloth, lower into boiling water
and simmer for 2 hours.

80. Steak and Kidney Pudding

Serves 4

1 lb (480 g) shin of
   beef
4 oz (120 g) pig's or
   lamb's kidney,
   sliced
1 tsp mixed dried
   herbs
salt, pepper
6 oz (180 g) onions,
   quartered

1 clove garlic,
   chopped
4 oz (120 g)
   mushrooms (or
   puffballs), chopped
suet pastry (as recipe
   no. 297) using 4 oz
   (120 g) suet and 8 oz
   (240 g) plain flour

Put beef, kidney, herbs and seasoning into a casserole;
well cover with water, put lid on, bring to the boil, then
cook overnight in a very slow oven. Next day, boil onion
and garlic in some of the liquor until tender (about 20
minutes). Line a well-greased pudding basin with two-
thirds of the pastry and fill with mixture of all cooked
ingredients and mushrooms or puffballs—plus 4 tbsps
liquor. (Use remaining liquor for gravy.) Moisten edge
of pastry and cover with pastry lid. Seal edge, make slit
in top and boil for $2\frac{1}{2}$ hours.

81. Thin Beef Pie   Serves 4

1 lb (480 g) minced
   beef
6 oz (180 g) onions,
   sliced
short pastry (as recipe
   no. 296) using 4 oz

(120 g) fat and 8 oz
(240 g) flour
1 tsp mixed dried
   herbs
salt, pepper
a little milk

Simmer beef for 30 minutes in $\frac{1}{2}$ pt (3 dl) water. Add
onions and continue cooking for 15 minutes. Line a pie
plate with half of the pastry and spoon beef and onions
into it (keeping back most of the liquor for gravy) and
sprinkle with herbs and seasoning. Moisten edge of
pastry and cover with pastry lid. Seal edge, brush with
milk, make a slit in top and bake in a moderately hot
oven for 30 minutes.

82. Beef and Vegetable Pie   Serves 4

1 lb (480 g) minced
   beef
6 oz (180 g) onions,
   grated
4 oz (120 g) parsnips,
   grated
4 oz (120 g) carrots,
   grated
4 oz (120 g) tomatoes,
   chopped
2 tbsps chopped
   parsley

1 tsp mixed dried
   herbs
short pastry (as recipe
   no. 296), using 3 oz
   (90 g) margarine,
   3 oz (90 g) lard and
   12 oz (360 g) self-
   raising flour
salt, pepper
a little milk

Line a greased pie dish with two-thirds of the pastry.
Mix together all other ingredients except milk. Turn
into pie dish, moisten edges of pastry and cover with
pastry lid. Seal edge, brush with milk, make slit in top
and bake in a hot oven for 10 minutes, then in a slow
oven for 2 hours.

83. Beef and Vegetable Pasties   *Makes 2*

6 oz (180 g) minced
   beef
plain pastry (as recipe
   no. 295), using 3 oz
   (90 g) fat and 8 oz
   (240 g) flour
$\frac{1}{2}$ oz (15 g) dripping
3 oz (90 g) onions,
   sliced
1 clove garlic,
   chopped

4 oz (120 g) potatoes,
   grated
4 oz (120 g) carrots,
   grated
$\frac{1}{2}$ tsp mixed dried
   herbs
pepper
$\frac{1}{2}$ tsp yeast extract
   dissolved in 2 tbsps
   hot water
a little milk

Divide pastry into two and roll each piece into a circle.
Melt dripping in a saucepan and gently fry onions and
garlic until soft but not brown. Add all other ingredients except yeast extract stock and milk. Mix well
together. Put lid on and cook gently for 10 minutes.
Remove from heat and stir in yeast extract stock. Put
half of the mixture on each pastry round. Draw up
opposite sides of pastry, moisten edges and press
together, fluting with the fingers. Brush with milk,
prick both sides with a fork and bake in a hot oven for 5
minutes, then in a slow oven for 50 minutes.

84. Cooked Meat Pasties   *Makes 2*

8 oz (240 g) cooked
   meat, cut small
6 oz (180 g) potatoes,
   grated
4 oz (120 g) onions,
   grated
½ tsp mixed dried
   herbs

salt, pepper
dash of Worcester-
   shire sauce
plain pastry (as recipe
   no. 295), using 3 oz
   (90 g) fat and 8 oz
   (240 g) flour
a little milk

Divide pastry into two and roll each piece into a circle.
Mix together all other ingredients except milk. Put half
of the mixture on each pastry round. Draw up opposite
sides of pastry, moisten edges and press together, fluting with the fingers. Brush with milk, prick both sides
with a fork and bake in a hot oven for 5 minutes, then in
a slow oven for 40 minutes.

85. Baked Pork Roll   *Serves 4*

12 oz (360 g) minced
   pork
suet pastry (as recipe
   no. 297), using 4 oz
   (120 g) suet and 8 oz
   (240 g) self-raising
   flour

8 oz (240 g) onions,
   grated
1 tsp mixed dried herbs
salt, pepper
a little milk

Roll out pastry into oblong. Mix together all other
ingredients, except milk, and spread over pastry.
Moisten edges and roll up. Seal edges, place on a well-
greased baking tray, brush with milk and bake in a hot
oven for 15 minutes, then in a slow oven for 1¼ hours.

86. Bacon Roly-poly

1 lb (480 g) streaky
  bacon
suet pastry (as recipe
  no. 297), using 4 oz
  (120 g) suet and 8 oz

(240 g) self-raising
  flour
1 tsp mixed dried herbs
4 tbsps chopped parsley
pepper

Fry bacon gently in own fat until partly cooked. Roll out
pastry into oblong and moisten edges. Lay bacon
rashers side by side on pastry and pour fat over.
Sprinkle on herbs, parsley and pepper, then roll up and
seal edges. Tie in a cloth, lower into boiling water and
simmer for 2 hours.

87. Bacon and Egg Pie

Serves 4

8 oz (240 g) streaky
  bacon
short pastry (as recipe
  no. 296), using 4 oz

(120 g) fat and 8 oz
  (240 g) flour
4 eggs
a little milk

Line a pie plate with two-thirds of the pastry. Lightly
fry bacon in own fat until cooked but not crisp, then
place in pie plate. Break eggs over (yolks evenly
spaced). Moisten edge of pastry, and cover with pastry
lid. Seal edge, brush with milk, make a slit in top and
bake in a moderately hot oven for 30 minutes.

88. Bacon and Egg Flan

Serves 4

8 oz (240 g) streaky
   bacon, cut small
plain pastry (as recipe
   no. 295), using 2 oz
   (60 g) margarine and
   5 oz (150 g) flour

2 eggs, beaten
$\frac{1}{2}$ pt (3 dl) milk
2 tbsps chopped chives
1 tbsp chopped parsley
pepper

Line an 8–9-in (20–22$\frac{1}{2}$-cm) flan tin with the pastry.
Fry bacon gently in own fat until cooked, but not crisp.
Beat eggs with milk, chives, parsley and seasoning.
Place bacon in flan tin, pour egg mixture over and bake
in a hot oven for 10 minutes, then in a slow oven for 30
to 40 minutes.

89. Bacon and Leek Pie

Serves 4

1 lb (480 g) streaky
   bacon, cut small
2 lb (960 g) leeks,
   chopped
1 egg
$\frac{1}{4}$ pt (1$\frac{1}{2}$ dl) milk
pepper

short pastry (as recipe
   no. 296), using 1$\frac{1}{2}$ oz
   (45 g) margarine,
   1$\frac{1}{2}$ oz (45 g) lard and
   6 oz (180 g) flour
a little extra milk

Simmer leeks until tender (about 20 minutes) then
drain. Fry bacon in own fat until cooked, but not crisp.
Turn leeks into bacon and mix well, then put into a
well-greased pie dish. Beat egg with milk and pepper
and pour into pie dish. Cover with pastry lid, brush
with milk, make a slit in top and bake in a moderately
hot oven until brown (20 to 30 minutes).

90. Bacon and Apple Pie Serves 4

12 oz (360 g) streaky bacon, cut small
8 oz (240 g) cooking apples, grated
4 oz (120 g) onions, grated
pepper

short pastry (as recipe no. 296), using $1\frac{1}{2}$ oz (45 g) margarine, $1\frac{1}{2}$ oz (45 g) lard and 6 oz (180 g) self-raising flour
a little milk

Fry bacon gently in own fat until cooked but not crisp. Mix apples with onions and pepper and put half of mixture in a well-greased pie dish. Place bacon on top and pour fat over. Put remaining apple mixture on top, then cover with pastry lid. Brush with milk, make a slit in top and bake in a hot oven for 5 minutes, then in a slow oven for 40 minutes.

91. Bacon and Cheese Pasties Makes 2

4 oz (120 g) boiled (or lightly fried) bacon, chopped
2 oz (60 g) cheese, grated
plain pastry (as recipe no. 295), using 3 oz (90 g) fat and 8 oz (240 g) flour

6 oz (180 g) onions, grated
4 oz (120 g) boiled potatoes, mashed
$\frac{1}{2}$ tsp mixed dried herbs
pepper
a little milk

Divide pastry into two and roll each piece into a circle. Mix together all other ingredients except milk. Put half of the mixture on each pastry round. Draw up opposite sides of pastry, moisten edges and press together, fluting with the fingers. Brush with milk, prick both sides with a fork and bake in a moderate oven until brown (20 to 30 minutes).

92. Sausage and Egg Pie

Serves 4

1 lb (480 g) sausage
  meat
2 eggs, hardboiled and
  quartered
salt, pepper
1 tsp mixed dried herbs

short pastry (as recipe
  no. 296), using 3 oz
  (90 g) margarine, 3 oz
  (90 g) lard and 12 oz
  (360 g) self-raising
  flour
a little milk

Line a pie dish with two-thirds of the pastry. Spread
half of the sausage meat over, sprinkle with herbs and
seasoning and arrange eggs. Spread remaining sausage meat on top, moisten edge of pastry and cover
with pastry lid. Seal edge, brush with milk, make a slit
in top and bake in a hot oven for 10 minutes, then in a
slow oven for 1 hour.

93. Rabbit Pie (1)

Serves 4

1 lb (480 g) rabbit pieces
8 oz (240 g) sausage
  meat
6 oz (180 g) onions,
  sliced
1 oz (30 g) dripping
1 tsp mixed dried herbs
salt, pepper

1 tsp yeast extract
  dissolved in $\frac{1}{4}$ pt
  $(1\frac{1}{2}$ dl) hot water
short pastry (as recipe
  no. 296), using $1\frac{1}{2}$ oz
  (45 g) margarine,
  $1\frac{1}{2}$ oz (45 g) lard
  and 6 oz (180 g)
  self-raising flour
a little milk

Simmer rabbit in water until tender (about 45 minutes).
Drain and leave to cool. Fry sausage meat and onions
in dripping (turning continuously) until partly cooked.
Pick rabbit meat from bones and mix with all other
ingredients except yeast extract stock, pastry and
milk. Fork into a greased pie dish. Pour yeast extract
stock over mixture. Cover with pastry lid, brush with
milk, make slit in top and bake in a moderate oven for
45 minutes.

94. Rabbit Pie (2)

$1\frac{1}{2}$ lb (720 g) rabbit
pieces
1 oz (30 g) dripping
4 oz (120 g) streaky
bacon, cut small
4 oz (120 g) onions,
sliced
1 dsp chopped
rosemary

2 tbsps chopped parsley
salt, pepper
short pastry (as recipe
no. 296), using $1\frac{1}{2}$ oz
(45 g) margarine,
$1\frac{1}{2}$ oz (45 g) lard and
6 oz (180 g) flour
a little milk

Melt dripping in a saucepan and cook rabbit, bacon
and onions for 5 minutes (turning occasionally). Add
rosemary, parsley and seasoning; cover with water
and simmer for 45 minutes. Remove from heat and
strain. Take out rabbit pieces and pick meat from
bones. Put back into saucepan, mix thoroughly then
turn into a pie dish, adding 3 or 4 tbsps liquor. Cover
with pastry lid, brush with milk, make slit in top and
bake in a moderate oven until brown (30 to 40 minutes).
(Use remaining liquor for gravy.)

95. Liver and Bacon Roly-poly

8 oz (240 g) pig's liver
6 oz (180 g) streaky
bacon
1 oz (30 g) dripping
6 oz (180 g) onions,
grated

1 tsp mixed dried herbs
salt, pepper
suet pastry (as recipe
no. 297), using 4 oz
(120 g) suet and 8 oz
(240 g) self-raising
flour

Fry liver and bacon in dripping until partly cooked,
then cut into small pieces. Roll out pastry into oblong
and moisten edges. Mix together all other ingredients
and spread over pastry. Roll up and seal edges. Tie in a
cloth, lower into boiling water and simmer for 2 hours.

3. Fish Dishes

A small stream runs through the garden at Hafod. Perhaps 'streamlet' describes this little watercourse more accurately because it is barely a couple of feet wide in places, and is fed only by a small spring. It tumbles down the slope in a series of pools and waterfalls, and supports a thriving community of life —including frogs, tadpoles, water spiders, beetles, water shrews and one newt. But an acquaintance of ours who had heard of, but not seen, our stream was convinced that only short-sightedness or lack of persistence on our part prevented us from retrieving brown trout or salmon from its waters. I wish he was right, because if you can't catch it yourself in these remote Welsh hills, you have to do without fresh fish—or trek to Conwy to await the arrival of the boats.

Mind you, the fish landed at Conwy is worth waiting for, and once upon a time at the beginning of the century (in the days of poverty, ignorance and deprivation) a hard-working man with a horse and cart used to bring fish from Conwy to sell to the moorland villagers the day after it had been brought ashore. Now (in these affluent, enlightened and civilized times) the only fish you can buy in the village is packeted frozen lumps of something that you take on trust as having, at one time, lived in the sea.

Fresh fish, as well as being difficult to obtain, has now become so expensive that it hardly warrants inclusion in a book of humble fare. With the lowly cod costing almost as much per pound as the trout, and the herring about to overtake the haddock, I now find myself frequently turning to recipes given to me by my mother—who knew better than most how to make a meal 'stretch'. A piece of fish that could easily be polished off by three people would be turned into a pie or fish cakes to serve six of us—and the following recipes are a few well-tried family favourites.

Most vegetable flavours combine well with fish (Jerusalem artichokes are particularly delicious) and I usually try to include a little lemon thyme when using mixed dried herbs.

96. Fish Pie

Serves 4

12 oz (360 g) cooked
  fish, boned and
  flaked
short pastry (as recipe
  no. 296), using 4 oz
  (120 g) suet and 8 oz
  (240 g) self-raising
  flour
2 hardboiled eggs,
  chopped

2 tbsps chopped parsley
pepper
white sauce (as recipe
  no. 305), using $\frac{1}{2}$ oz
  (15 g) butter, $\frac{1}{2}$ oz
  (15 g) flour and $\frac{1}{4}$ pt
  (1 $\frac{1}{2}$ dl) milk
a little milk

Line a well-greased pie dish with two-thirds of the
pastry. Fill the dish with a mixture of fish, eggs,
parsley and pepper. Pour the white sauce over, then
cover with pastry, sealing edges. Brush with milk,
make a slit in the middle and bake in a hot oven for 15
minutes, then in a slow oven for a further 20 minutes.

97. Fish Roly-poly

Serves 4

12 oz (360 g) cooked
  fish, boned and
  flaked
suet pastry (as recipe
  no. 297), using 4 oz
  (120 g) suet and 8 oz
  (240 g) self-raising
  flour

2 tsps mixed dried
  herbs
salt, pepper
Worcestershire sauce
2 tbsps chopped parsley
a little plain flour

Roll pastry into oblong and moisten edges. Mix fish
with all other ingredients except flour. Spread the mixture on the pastry and roll up, pressing the edges
together. Tie in a well-floured cloth (allowing room for
expansion) and lower into boiling water. Simmer for 2
hours.

98. Fish Hot Pot
Serves 4

1 lb (480 g) any fish,
  divided into 4 pieces
1 oz (30 g) dripping
6 oz (180 g) carrots,
  chopped
4 oz (120 g) onions,
  chopped
4 tbsps chopped parsley

6 oz (180 g) tomatoes,
  sliced
salt, pepper
2 lb (960 g) potatoes,
  thinly sliced
$\frac{1}{4}$ pt (1 $\frac{1}{2}$ dl) milk
1 oz (30 g) butter

Melt dripping in a saucepan and cook carrots and onions gently for about 5 minutes. Put half the tomatoes in a well-greased, ovenproof dish and cover with the carrot and onion mixture. Sprinkle parsley over, then add fish, remainder of tomatoes, seasoning and finally the potatoes. Pour milk over, dot with butter, put on lid (or cover with foil) and cook in a moderately hot oven for 1 hour. Remove the lid or foil and cook until top is golden brown (about 15 minutes).

99. Fish Soufflé (1)
Serves 4

8 oz (240 g) cooked fish,
  boned and flaked
3 oz (90 g) breadcrumbs
$\frac{1}{4}$ pt (1 $\frac{1}{2}$ dl) milk

$\frac{1}{2}$ tsp yeast extract
pepper
4 tbsps chopped parsley
2 eggs, separated

Mix fish with breadcrumbs. Warm milk and stir in yeast extract. Add pepper and parsley, then pour over fish mixture. Add egg yolks to fish mixture and mix well together. Beat egg whites until stiff and fold into mixture. Turn into a well-greased pie dish and cook in a moderately hot oven for about 20 minutes.

100. Fish Soufflé (2)   Serves 4

8 oz (240 g) cooked fish,   3 eggs, separated
   boned and flaked   2 oz (60 g) breadcrumbs
1 oz (30 g) butter $\frac{1}{2}$ tsp Worcestershire
1 oz (30 g) plain flour   sauce
$\frac{1}{4}$ pt (1 $\frac{1}{2}$ dl) milk

Melt butter in a saucepan. Remove from heat then stir
in flour smoothly. Add milk slowly, stirring to prevent
lumps. Return to heat and cook gently for a few
minutes, stirring continuously. Remove from heat, add
egg yolks, breadcrumbs, sauce and fish. Mix well. Beat
egg whites until stiff and fold into mixture. Turn into a
well-greased pie dish and cook in a moderately hot
oven for about 25 minutes.

101. Fish and Macaroni Pie   Serves 4

12 oz (360 g) cooked   white sauce (as recipe
   fish, boned and   no. 305), using $\frac{1}{2}$ oz
   flaked   (15 g) butter, $\frac{1}{2}$ oz
6 oz (180 g) cooked   (15 g) flour and $\frac{1}{4}$ pt
   macaroni, chopped   (1 $\frac{1}{2}$ dl) milk
6 oz (180 g) tomatoes,   4 tbsps breadcrumbs
   sliced   2 oz (60 g) cheese,
                     grated

Mix together fish, macaroni and tomatoes, then turn
into a greased pie dish. Pour white sauce over, then
sprinkle with breadcrumbs and top with cheese. Bake
in a hot oven for 30 minutes.

102. Fish and Macaroni Casserole   *Serves 4*

1 lb (480 g) any fish,
   divided into 4 pieces
2 oz (60 g) macaroni,
   broken short
4 tbsps chopped parsley
2 tsps mixed dried
   herbs

salt, pepper
4 oz (120 g) bread-
   crumbs
2 eggs
$\frac{1}{4}$ pt (1 $\frac{1}{2}$ dl) milk
a little butter

Put macaroni into boiling water and partially cook it,
for about 15 minutes, then strain. Put fish into bottom
of a casserole. Mix macaroni with parsley, herbs and
seasoning and spread over fish. Cover with breadcrumbs. Beat up eggs, add milk, and pour into casserole. Dot with small pieces of butter and cook (with
lid on) in moderately hot oven for 1 hour. Remove lid
and cook until top is golden-brown (about 10 minutes).

103. Fish and Jerusalem Artichoke Pie   *Serves 4*

12 oz (360 g) cooked
   fish, boned and
   flaked
12 oz (360 g) Jerusalem
   artichokes, boiled
   and mashed
white sauce (as recipe
   no. 305), using $\frac{1}{2}$ oz
   (15 g) butter,

$\frac{1}{2}$ oz (15 g) flour and
   $\frac{1}{4}$ pt (1 $\frac{1}{2}$ dl) milk
pepper
4 tbsps chopped parsley
1 $\frac{1}{2}$ lb (720 g) potatoes,
   boiled and mashed
   with a little butter,
   milk, salt and
   sprinkle of nutmeg

Mix together fish, artichokes, white sauce and pepper,
then turn into a greased pie dish. Mix parsley with
potato and spread on top. Bake in a hot oven until
golden-brown (20 to 30 minutes).

104. Jerusalem Artichoke Fish Cakes   Makes 8–10

8 oz (240 g) cooked fish,
  boned and flaked
8 oz (240 g) Jerusalem
  artichokes, boiled
8 oz (240 g) potatoes,
  boiled

2 oz (60 g) cheese,
  grated
salt, pepper
plain flour for coating
fat for frying

Mash together all ingredients except flour and fat.
With floured hands make into little flat cakes, coat
with flour and fry on both sides until golden-brown.

105. Haddock Pie (1)   Serves 4

12 oz (360 g) cooked
  smoked haddock,
  boned and flaked
1 oz (30 g) butter
3 tbsps rice, boiled
6 oz (180 g) cooking
  apples, grated

6 oz (180 g) onions,
  grated
1 dsp chutney
pepper

Melt butter and mix well with all other ingredients.
Turn into a well-greased pie dish, cover with foil and
bake in a moderate oven for 45 minutes.

106. Haddock Pie (2)   Serves 4

12 oz (360 g) cooked
  fresh haddock, boned
  and flaked
white sauce (as recipe
  no. 305), using $\frac{1}{2}$ oz
  (15 g) butter, $\frac{1}{2}$ oz
  (15 g) flour and $\frac{1}{4}$ pt
  (1 $\frac{1}{2}$ dl) milk

2 tbsps chopped parsley
1 $\frac{1}{2}$ lb (720 g) potatoes,
  boiled and mashed
  with a little butter
  and milk
2 oz (60 g) cheese,
  grated

Mix together fish, white sauce and parsley. Make a
border of mashed potato around a pie dish. Pour fish
mixture into centre. Sprinkle cheese over all and bake
in a hot oven until golden brown (about 30 minutes).

107. Stuffed Herrings   Serves 4

4 herrings, filleted
4 herring roes
2 oz (60 g) breadcrumbs
4 oz (120 g) onions (or
   shallots) chopped

1 tsp mixed dried herbs
a little Worcestershire
   sauce
salt, pepper
2 oz (60 g) butter

Cook roes in a little water for about 15 minutes. Drain
and mix with half of the butter and all other ingredients except fish. Place 4 halves of herring side by
side in a well-greased, ovenproof dish. Spread mixture
on them, then lay the other fish halves on top. Smear
tops of fish with remaining butter. Cover with grease-
proof paper or foil and bake in a moderate oven for
about 20 minutes.

108. Herring Fish Cakes   Makes 2 – 3

1 herring, boiled, boned
   and flaked
3 tbsps breadcrumbs
1 egg, beaten
$\frac{1}{2}$ tsp mixed dried herbs
salt, pepper

1 tsp Worcestershire
   sauce
1 tbsp chopped parsley
plain flour for coating
fat for frying

Mix together all ingredients except flour and fat. With
floured hands make into little flat cakes, coat with
flour and fry on both sides until golden-brown.

109. Herring Roe Pie

Serves 4

12 oz (360 g) herring
    roes
2 tsps vinegar
6 oz (180 g)
    breadcrumbs

4 tbsps chopped parsley
salt, pepper
2 oz (60 g) butter

Simmer roes in $\frac{1}{4}$ pt ($1\frac{1}{2}$ dl) water with vinegar added for 15 minutes. Strain. Fill a well-greased pie dish with alternate layers of herring roes and a mixture of breadcrumbs, parsley and seasoning, finishing with the mixture. Dot top liberally with butter and bake in a moderately hot oven until browned (about 20 minutes).

110. Herring Roe Snack

Enough for 4 slices of toast

4 oz (120 g) herring roes
    (soft, hard or a
    mixture)
$\frac{1}{4}$ pt ($1\frac{1}{2}$ dl) milk
$\frac{1}{2}$ oz (15 g) butter

$\frac{1}{2}$ oz (15 g) plain flour
2 tbsps breadcrumbs
1 dsp chopped parsley
salt, pepper

Simmer roes in milk until cooked (about 20 minutes). Drain off milk and put aside. Melt butter in a small saucepan, stir in flour. Remove from heat and gradually add the saved milk, stirring continuously. Stir in all other ingredients, mixing well together. Return to heat and simmer until mixture is thick enough to pile on toast.

111. Stuffed Mackerel

Serves 4

4 mackerel, filleted
2 oz (60 g) butter
4 oz (120 g)
  breadcrumbs
4 oz (120 g) onions (or
  shallots) chopped

2 tsps dried thyme
2 dsps chopped chives
cayenne pepper, salt

Melt half the butter and mix with all other ingredients except fish. Place 4 halves of mackerel side by side in a well-greased, ovenproof dish. Spread mixture on them, then lay the other fish halves on top, Smear tops of fish with remaining butter. Cover with greaseproof paper or foil and bake in moderate oven for 20 to 30 minutes.

112. Pilchard Pie (or Fish Cakes)

Serves 4

1 15-oz (or 425 g) can
  pilchards
2 lb (960 g) potatoes,
  boiled and mashed
4 oz (120 g)
  breadcrumbs

2 tsps mixed dried
  herbs
4 tbsps chopped parsley
Worcestershire sauce
salt, pepper

Mix all ingredients together. Turn into a greased pie dish and brown under a hot grill or in a hot oven.

VARIATION: For *Pilchard Fish Cakes*, make mixture into little flat cakes with floured hands, coat with plain flour and fry until browned on both sides.

113. Sardine Pasties   *Makes 2*

1 small can sardines,
   drained
plain pastry (as recipe
   no. 295), using 3 oz
   (90 g) fat and 8 oz
   (240 g) flour

6 oz (180 g) potatoes,
   boiled and mashed
$\frac{1}{2}$ tsp mixed dried herbs
1 tbsp chopped chives
salt, pepper
a little milk

Divide pastry into two and shape each piece into a circle. Mix together all other ingredients except milk. Put half of the mixture on each pastry round. Draw up opposite sides of pastry, moisten edges and press together, fluting with the fingers. Brush with milk, prick both sides with a fork and bake in a moderately hot oven until golden-brown (20 to 30 minutes).

4. Vegetable, Cheese and Egg Dishes

Top of stove dishes
114. Vegetable Roly-poly
115. Fresh Herb Pudding
116. Carrot and Rice Savoury
117. Jerusalem Artichoke Savoury
118. Onion and Cheese Savoury
119. Toasted Onion Squares
120. Parsnip and Nut Rissoles
121. Potato Rissoles
122. Potato and Onion Drop Scones
123. Boiled Swede and Potato
124. Sweetcorn Drop Scones
125. Tomato and Macaroni Rissoles
126. Turnip and Cauliflower Savoury
127. Vegetable Marrow Grill
128. Butter Bean Fritters
129. Lentil Curry
130. Lentil Rolls
131. Lentil and Egg Rissoles
132. Lentil and Rice Puffs
133. Oat Rissoles
134. Chanterelle Omelette
135. Puffballs in Sauce
136. Eggs in Cheese Jackets

Oven dishes
137. Vegetable and Lentil Casserole
138. Vegetable and Haricot Bean Pie
139. Leftover Vegetable Soufflé
140. Dried Herb Pudding
141. Beetroot and Cheese Bake
142. Cabbage and Cheese Bake
143. Cauliflower Hot Pot
144. Cauliflower Pie
145. Ted and Daisy's Cauliflower Cheese

Pudding
146. French Bean and Egg Savoury
147. Fungus Soufflé
148. Jerusalem Artichoke Soufflé
149. Leek and Soya Savoury
150. Parsnip and Nut Soufflé
151. Pea and Tomato (September) Hot Pot
152. Potato and Nut Soufflé
153. Spinach and Cheese Savoury
154. Spinach and Lentils with Cheese
155. Tomato and Cheese Savoury
156. Tomato and Haricot Bean Cheese Bake
157. Turnip Pie
158. Turnip and Lentil Bake
159. Vegetable Marrow and Butter Bean Bake
160. Butter Bean Roast
161. Dried Pea and Cheese Pie

162. Lentil Roast
163. Lentil and Walnut Roast
164. Lentil Savoury
165. Lentil and Cheese Pie
166. Nut Roast
167. Rice and Cheese Savoury
168. Egg and Cheese Pie
169. Bread and Cheese Pudding
170. Cheese Pudding
171. Bread and Cheese Soufflé
172. Poor Man's Cheese Soufflé
173. Cheese and Butter Bean Flan
174. Cheese and Carrot Flan
175. Cheese and Onion Flan (1)
176. Cheese and Onion Flan (2)
177. Cheese and Egg Pasties
178. Cheese and Onion Pasties
179. Vegetable Pie with Cheese Pastry

TOP OF STOVE DISHES

There can be few blessings more comforting than that of having rights to a plot of land in which to grow vegetables. No one who plans their garden carefully need be without fresh vegetables, and at Hafod we tried to make sure that whatever the season it was always possible to wander out into the garden and find something to eat.

At the end of winter, when the last of the parsnips, carrots and swedes had been eaten, then the chickweed, lambs lettuce and fresh parsley were ready to give us salads—and the kale was still there to help us over the 'hungry gap' of April and May. In summer the garden was in full production, with spinach and seakale beet, carrots, lettuces, peas, beans, and beetroot for the picking, In the autumn we lifted the potatoes and took our first pickings from the new kale plants. With any luck, the sprouts would be ready for Christmas. We always kept back some peas to dry for winter stores, and potatoes and carrots were stored away for food during the darkest days—but, generally speaking, we ate our vegetables in their season of growing, and so our diet changed quite naturally with the passing of the months.

A dish of freshly picked young vegetables—raw, or lightly cooked—or a potato baked in its jacket, needs little to accompany it other than a grating of cheese or some butter. Alternatively, if you prefer a more savoury flavour, try a dish of fried onions, cooked in dripping, thickened with a little plain flour and yeast extract, and with water from the vegetables added to make a gravy. Serve this as a rich tasty sauce over new potatoes, young peas and carrots. Nothing could be more appetizing. But when there is a glut of a particular vegetable, or when the vegetables are at the end of their season, or are taken from store, then I like to mix them with herbs, or combine them with dried pulses, cheese or egg to make tasty and nourishing meals.

My storecupboard has always contained a goodly supply of dried pulses—and this was particularly important during the winter at Hafod when we knew that we could be cut off from the outside world for weeks at a time. Blizzards would sometimes last for days on end—and under these conditions waist-high snowdrifts would block the road—the open moorland became a featureless antarctic landscape—and our vegetable garden would be buried beneath several feet of snow. If we were not well-provisioned we would starve . . . and stocking up the cupboard was the most important autumn task. Having organized my preserves, canned food, flour and oatmeal—and gathered as many hazel nuts as I could find—I set about replenishing my supplies of dried pulses. Here, surely, is the best way of storing protein against hard times; haricot beans (to add to stews and pies), butter beans (delicious with boiled bacon and parsley sauce) and, of course, lentils. Perhaps lentils are our favourite dried pulse because they need no overnight soaking, nor long cooking, and their delightful peppery flavour is a welcome addition to soups, stews, casseroles, rissoles and baked dishes.

Dried pulses, herbs, nuts and cereals combined with other vegetables are used in the recipes throughout the following two sections, but in the first part all dishes can be cooked on top of the stove, and most of them are quick to prepare.

114. Vegetable Roly-poly   *Serves 4*

10 oz (300 g) mixed root
   vegetables, grated
suet pastry (as recipe
   no. 297), using 4 oz
   (120 g) suet and 8 oz
   (240 g) self-raising
   flour
$\frac{1}{2}$ tsp yeast extract

4 oz (120 g) onions,
   chopped
4 oz (120 g) tomatoes,
   chopped
3 tbsps chopped parsley
1 tsp mixed dried herbs
pepper

Roll out pastry into oblong and spread yeast extract over. Cover with mixture of all other ingredients. Moisten edges and roll up. Seal edges, tie in a cloth, lower into pan of boiling water and simmer for $2\frac{1}{2}$ hours.

115. Fresh Herb Pudding   *Serves 4*

2 tbsps chopped parsley
2 tbsps chopped sage
2 tbsps chopped thyme
2 tbsps chopped
  marjoram
$\frac{1}{4}$ pt (1 $\frac{1}{2}$ dl) milk
2 oz (60 g) dripping
1 tsp yeast extract

scraps of bread to fill
  2-pt (12-dl) basin,
  soaked in water for a
  few hours (or
  overnight)
12 oz (360 g) onions,
  grated
2 eggs, beaten
1 tbsp oatmeal
pepper

Heat milk together with dripping and yeast extract.
Drain bread and squeeze dry. Mix all ingredients
together, then turn into a greased 2-pt (12-dl) pudding
basin. Boil for 2 hours.

116. Carrot and Rice Savoury   *Serves 4*

1 lb (480 g) carrots,
  grated
2 oz (60 g) rice
1 tsp yeast extract
cayenne pepper

$\frac{1}{2}$ oz (15 g) butter
2 tbsps chopped chives
2 oz (60 g) cheese,
  grated

Put carrots in pan with $\frac{1}{2}$ pt (3 dl) water. Bring to the
boil, then add rice, yeast extract and cayenne pepper.
Simmer until rice is cooked and all water absorbed
(about 30 minutes). Stir in butter, chives and half of the
cheese, then turn into a greased, ovenproof dish.
Sprinkle with rest of cheese and grill until cheese is
brown.

117. Jerusalem Artichoke Savoury

1 lb (480 g) Jerusalem
  artichokes, cut small
1 lb (480 g) potatoes
½ oz (15 g) butter
½ oz (15 g) plain flour

2 tbsps milk
2 tbsps chopped parsley
salt, pepper
2 oz (60 g) cheese,
  grated

Boil artichokes until tender (about 20 minutes). Meanwhile boil potatoes and keep hot. Melt butter in a saucepan, remove from heat and blend with flour, then gradually stir in milk. Make up to ¼ pt (1½ dl) with artichoke liquor and cook slowly until sauce thickens. Stir in parsley and seasoning. Line a well-greased pie dish with the drained and mashed potatoes, then fill with the drained artichokes. Pour sauce over and sprinkle with cheese. Grill until cheese is brown and bubbling.

118. Onion and Cheese Savoury

6 oz (180 g) cheese,
  grated
10 oz (300 g) onions,
  quartered
2 lb (960 g) potatoes,
  diced

4 tbsps chopped parsley
cayenne pepper
3 small tomatoes,
  halved
a little butter

Simmer onions and potatoes until cooked, then drain and mash. Stir in 5 oz (150 g) cheese, parsley and cayenne pepper. Turn into a warmed ovenproof dish and press tomatoes (cut side up) into mixture. Dot tomatoes with butter, sprinkle remaining cheese over, and grill until brown on top.

119. Toasted Onion Squares   Serves 4

8 oz (240 g) onions, sliced	a little dripping
fat for frying	a little made mustard
4 thick slices bread	4 slices cheese to cover bread

Fry onions gently until cooked and lightly browned.
Toast bread lightly and spread generously with dripping. Place onions evenly over toast. Spread mustard
on cheese and place (mustard-side down) on onions.
Grill until cheese is brown and bubbling.

120. Parsnip and Nut Rissoles   Makes 10–12

12 oz (360 g) parsnips, diced	2 tbsps breadcrumbs
2 oz (60 g) nuts, chopped	salt, pepper
$\frac{1}{2}$ oz (15 g) butter	a little plain flour
	fat for frying

Simmer parsnips until tender (about 20 minutes),
drain, then mash with butter. Mix with nuts, breadcrumbs and seasoning. Leave to cool, then with floured
hands make into little flat cakes. Coat with flour and
fry each side until brown.

121. Potato Rissoles   Makes 12–14

1 lb (480 g) boiled potatoes, mashed	1 tsp mixed dried herbs
5 oz (150 g) onions, grated	salt, pepper
1 egg, beaten	a little plain flour
	fat for frying

Mix all ingredients together except flour and fat. With
floured hands make into little flat cakes and fry each
side until brown.

122. Potato and Onion Drop Scones   Makes 10–12

8 oz (240 g) potato,
   grated
8 oz (240 g) onions,
   grated
2 eggs

3 tbsps plain flour
$\frac{1}{4}$ pt (1 $\frac{1}{2}$ dl) milk
salt, pepper
fat for frying

Beat eggs, gradually adding flour, then stir in all other
ingredients except fat. Beat well, then drop tablespoons of mixture into a hot, greased pan and fry each
side gently until brown.

123. Boiled Swede and Potato (Stwnch)   Serves 4

1 lb (480 g) swedes,
   diced
1 lb (480 g) potatoes
2 oz (60 g) butter

2 tbsps top of the milk
2 tbsps chopped parsley
salt, pepper

Boil swedes and potatoes together, strain and mash.
Mix all ingredients together and beat well.

124. Sweetcorn Drop Scones   Makes 8–10

1 small can sweetcorn,
   drained
2 eggs
3 tbsps plain flour

2 tbsps chopped chives
salt, pepper
fat for frying

Beat eggs, gradually adding flour, then stir in all other
ingredients except fat. Beat well, then drop tablespoons of mixture into a hot, greased pan and fry each
side gently until brown.

125. Tomato and Macaroni Rissoles   Makes 10–12

4 oz (120 g) macaroni
4 oz (120 g) onions,
  sliced
4 oz (120 g) tomatoes,
  sliced
fat for frying

4 oz (120 g)
  breadcrumbs
1 egg, beaten
1 tsp mixed dried herbs
cayenne pepper, salt
a little plain flour

Drop macaroni into boiling water and cook until slightly soft (about 15 minutes) then drain and chop small. Fry onions and tomatoes gently until soft but not brown. Mix together all ingredients except fat and flour. Leave to cool, then with floured hands make into little flat cakes, coat with flour and fry each side until crisp and brown.

126. Turnip and Cauliflower Savoury   Serves 4

2 medium turnips,
  unpeeled
1 small cauliflower (an
  old one with useless
  leaves is suitable),
  cut into sprigs
cayenne pepper, salt
cheese sauce (as recipe
  no. 306), using 3 oz
  (90 g) cheese,

$\frac{1}{2}$ oz (15 g) butter, 3 oz
(90 g) onions, 3 oz
(90 g) tomatoes, 1 egg,
3 tbsps milk, cayenne
pepper and 1 dsp
chopped chives
1 oz (30 g) grated
cheese, mixed with
2 oz (60 g)
breadcrumbs

Boil turnips until almost cooked (about 30 minutes), then drain. Meanwhile boil cauliflower sprigs separately until almost cooked (about 15 minutes) then drain. When cool enough to handle, peel and slice turnips, then arrange with cauliflower sprigs in a greased, ovenproof dish. Season and pour cheese sauce over. Sprinkle with cheese and breadcrumb mixture, then grill until brown on top.

127. Vegetable Marrow Grill

Serves 4

½ medium marrow, cut
  into rings, then
  quartered
10 oz (300 g) onions,
  quartered
4 oz (120 g) carrots, cut
  into rounds
white sauce (recipe no.
  305), using 1 oz (30 g)
  butter,

1 oz (30 g) flour and
  ½ pt (3 dl) milk
3 oz (90 g) cheese,
  grated
½ tsp dry mustard
salt, pepper
2 oz (60 g) breadcrumbs
a little butter

Boil vegetables until tender (about 20 minutes). Stir half the cheese, with the mustard and seasoning, into the white sauce. Arrange vegetables in a warm, shallow, ovenproof dish and pour sauce over. Mix remaining cheese with breadcrumbs and sprinkle on top. Dot with butter and grill until crisp and brown on top.

128. Butter Bean Fritters

Makes 8–10

5 oz (150 g) butter
  beans, soaked
  overnight
2 oz (60 g) breadcrumbs
1 egg, beaten
2 tbsps chopped parsley

1 dsp chopped
  rosemary
salt, pepper
a little plain flour
butter for frying

Simmer butter beans until soft (about 2 hours—adding water if necessary). Drain and mash with all other ingredients except flour and butter. Leave to cool, then with floured hands make into little flat cakes, coat with flour and fry each side until brown.

129. Lentil Curry   *Serves 4*

8 oz (240 g) lentils
1 dsp curry powder
1 oz (30 g) fat
8 oz (240 g) onions,
  chopped
1 clove garlic, chopped

6 oz (180 g) apples,
  chopped
2 bananas, sliced
1 oz (30 g) sultanas
1 dsp chutney
salt

Melt fat in a saucepan and fry onions, garlic and apples gently for 5 minutes, then stir in curry powder, lentils and 1 pt (6 dl) water. Put lid on and simmer for 30 minutes. Add all other ingredients and continue cooking for 15 minutes, stirring continuously.

130. Lentil Rolls   *Makes 10 – 12*

6 oz (180 g) lentils
6 oz (180 g) onions,
  chopped small
fat for frying
4 oz (120 g) boiled
  potatoes

2 oz (60 g) breadcrumbs
1 tsp mixed dried herbs
$\frac{1}{2}$ tsp yeast extract
a little oatmeal

Simmer lentils gently in about $\frac{1}{2}$ pt (3 dl) water for about 20 minutes, stirring occasionally. (All water must be absorbed, but it may be necessary to add some during cooking.) Fry onions gently until tender but not brown. Mash together all ingredients except fat and oatmeal. Leave to cool, then make into 10 or 12 sausage-shaped rolls. Coat with oatmeal and fry until brown all over.

131. Lentil and Egg Rissoles   Makes 10–12

6 oz (180 g) lentils
2 hardboiled eggs,
    chopped
5 oz (150 g) onions,
    chopped

fat for frying
2 tbsps chopped parsley
$\frac{1}{2}$ tsp grated nutmeg
salt, pepper
a little plain flour

Simmer lentils in $\frac{1}{2}$ pt (3 dl) water for about 20 minutes,
stirring occasionally. (All water must be absorbed but
it may be necessary to add some during cooking.) Fry
onions gently until soft but not brown. Mix together all
ingredients except flour and fat; leave to cool then with
floured hands make into little flat cakes. Coat with
flour and fry each side until brown.

132. Lentil and Rice Puffs   Makes 12–14

4 oz (120 g) lentils
2 oz (60 g) rice
1 tsp yeast extract
6 oz (180 g) onions,
    chopped
fat for frying
2 oz (60 g) cheese,
    grated
1 egg yolk
$\frac{1}{2}$ tsp dry mustard
salt, pepper

For the batter
4 oz (120 g) plain flour
1 tbsp oil
$\frac{1}{4}$ pt (1 $\frac{1}{2}$ dl) warm water
salt, pepper
1 egg white, beaten
    stiffly
deep fat for frying

Simmer lentils and rice together with yeast extract in
about $\frac{3}{4}$ pt (4$\frac{1}{2}$ dl) water for about 20 minutes, stirring
occasionally. (All water must be absorbed but it may
be necessary to add some during cooking.) Fry onions
gently for 5 minutes then mix with all other ingredients
except batter and fat, and leave to cool.

Blend flour with oil and gradually add warm water
to make smooth batter. Stir in seasoning then fold in
egg white. With floured hands make lentil mixture into
little balls, coat with batter and fry in deep boiling fat
until golden brown (about 5 minutes).

133. Oat Rissoles

4 oz (120 g) oatmeal
4 oz (120 g) onions,
  grated
1 egg, beaten
1 oz (30 g) cheese,
  grated
2 tbsps chopped parsley

1 tsp mixed dried herbs
salt, pepper
dash of Worcestershire
  sauce
a little plain flour
dripping for frying

Boil ½ pt (3 dl) water, then add oatmeal and simmer until thick, stirring occasionally. Leave to cool, then beat in all other ingredients except flour and dripping. With floured hands make into little flat cakes, coat with flour and fry in dripping until golden-brown on each side.

134. Chanterelle Omelette

Serves 2

6 oz (180 g)
  chanterelles,
  quartered
2 oz (60 g) onions (or
  shallots), chopped

fat for frying
4 eggs
2 tbsps chopped parsley
salt, pepper

Fry chanterelles and onions (or shallots) gently until tender. Beat eggs with parsley and seasoning and pour over chanterelle and onion mixture. Increase heat and after 3 minutes divide omelette in two. Turn each half carefully to cook the other side.

(Chanterelle—also known as 'Egg Sponge'—is easily recognized by its yolk-of-egg colour and wavy funnel shape. It smells very faintly of apricots, and doesn't need peeling. Found in woodlands during summer and autumn.)

135. Puffballs in Sauce

This is an ideal way of cooking tiny puffballs.

puffballs, halved
milk to cover
a little butter (see
method)

a little plain flour (see
method)
chives to taste
a little grated nutmeg
salt, pepper

Simmer puffballs in enough milk to cover, until soft (a few minutes). Strain off milk, measure it, and leave to cool. Melt butter ($\frac{1}{2}$ oz (15 g) to each $\frac{1}{4}$ pt (1$\frac{1}{2}$ dl) milk) in a saucepan, then remove from heat and stir in flour ($\frac{1}{2}$ oz (15 g) to each $\frac{1}{4}$ pt (1$\frac{1}{2}$ dl) milk). Then gradually stir in cooled milk. Return to heat, stirring continuously until thick. Add puffballs and all other ingredients and continue cooking gently for a few minutes.

(Puffballs (there are many species—all edible) are usually found in grassland and are best eaten young in summer. They are smooth, creamy white and have no noticeable stem. They do not need to be peeled.)

136. Eggs in Cheese Jackets (Welsh Eggs)   Makes 4

4 small eggs, hardboiled
6 oz (180 g) cheese,
grated
3 oz (90 g) plain flour

cayenne pepper, salt
2 tbsps milk
a little oatmeal
deep fat for frying

Mix together cheese, flour and seasoning. Stir in milk and mix well. With wet hands cover hardboiled eggs with mixture. Coat with oatmeal and fry in deep fat until brown (about 5 minutes).

OVEN DISHES

You will already have noticed that we like cheese. We manage without meat quite happily for most of the

102

week, but cheese, so far as we are concerned, is a staple food. And by cheese we mean, usually, Cheddar cheese. Certainly we like occasional bits of Danish Blue, Stilton or Austrian smoked cheese, but to us these are just *fun* cheeses. Not real food.

We were amazed when we moved to Wales to find that the locals did not share our reverence for Cheddar cheese. Cheddar cheese was a joke, they said. 'Mouse trap' cheese, they called it. So, in retaliation, I feel I am permitted to be rude about the cheeses of Hiraethog. There are two kinds. Each cheese is disc-shaped and enfolded in plastic sheeting; the one called 'caws gwyn' (white cheese) and the other 'caws coch' (red cheese). Ask for Cheshire, Wensleydale or Lancashire, and you will be offered caws gwyn. Demand Double Gloucester or Leicester and you will come away carrying caws coch. No one admits to stocking Caerphilly. But on one occasion I really thought that I had found a grocer to supply me with Cheddar cheese. 'Certainly, Madam,' he said, bringing out a familiar looking plastic covered disc, 'would you like white Cheddar or red?'

It didn't take us long to come to terms with the fact that losing Cheddar cheese was the price we had to pay for the privilege of living in the hills, and I found that all my favourite cheese dishes could in fact be made with caws gwyn or coch (it didn't matter which—they taste the same) without much noticeable difference in the final result.

The timing of the soufflés is important if you are fussy about their puffy appearance, but if you want a soufflé that will stand a bit of ill-treatment, try recipe no. 171. This is an adaptation of a recipe given to me by my sister-in-law who is a school cook-in-charge. School dinners, would you believe it, are often carted from one side of the city to the other—and recipe no. 171 is guaranteed to stand up to this sort of treatment because the breadcrumbs prevent it from sinking.

137. Vegetable and Lentil Casserole Serves 4

2 lb (960 g) mixed
   vegetables (including
   onion and 1 clove
   garlic), cut small
4 oz (120 g) lentils
1 oz (30 g) dripping

2 tbsps chopped parsley
1 tsp mixed dried herbs
1 tsp yeast extract
pepper
1 tbsp plain flour

Melt dripping in a saucepan and gently cook mixed vegetables for 15 minutes, stirring occasionally. Turn into a casserole, cover with water and stir in all other ingredients except flour. Put lid on and cook in a moderate oven for 2 hours. (After 1 hour add more water if necessary.) Make a paste of flour and a little water, then thin down with liquor from casserole. Add this to casserole and stir well. Replace lid and cook for a further 15 minutes.

Alternatively, this meal can be cooked in a stewpan on top of the stove.

138. Vegetable and Haricot Bean Pie Serves 4

3 tbsps haricot beans,
   soaked overnight
1 lb (480 g) mixed root
   vegetables, cut small
8 oz (240 g) onions,
   chopped
1 clove garlic, chopped
$1\frac{1}{2}$ oz (45 g) butter
4 tbsps chopped parsley

white sauce (as recipe
   no. 305), using $\frac{1}{2}$ oz
   (15 g) butter, $\frac{1}{2}$ oz
   (15 g) flour and $\frac{1}{4}$ pt
   ($1\frac{1}{2}$ dl) milk
$1\frac{1}{2}$ lb (720 g) boiled
   potatoes
a little milk
salt, pepper

Simmer beans until soft (about $1\frac{1}{2}$ hours). Melt butter in a saucepan and cook root vegetables, onions and garlic gently with lid on for 20 minutes. Then add beans and parsley. Mix well, turn into a greased pie dish and pour white sauce over. Mash potatoes with milk and seasoning, then fork into the pie dish. Bake in a hot oven until brown (20 to 30 minutes).

139. Leftover Vegetable Soufflé   *Serves 4*

1 lb (480 g) mixed
   cooked vegetables,
   diced
4 tbsps chopped chives
$\frac{1}{2}$ tsp dry mustard

white sauce (as recipe
   no. 305), adding 2 oz
   (60 g) cheese, grated
2 eggs, separated

Put vegetables, chives and mustard into a well-greased
pie dish. Pour over half the cheese sauce. Blend egg
yolks with remainder of cheese sauce. Beat whites of
eggs until stiff, then fold into cheese sauce and pour
over vegetables. Bake in a moderately hot oven for 25
minutes.

140. Dried Herb Pudding   *Serves 4*

1 tsp dried sage
1 dsp dried thyme
1 dsp dried marjoram
1 dsp dried balm
8 oz (240 g) bread (fresh
   or stale)

12 oz (360 g) onions,
   sliced
1 oz (30 g) dripping
3 oz (90 g) suet
salt, pepper
1 egg, beaten
$\frac{1}{4}$ pt (1 $\frac{1}{2}$ dl) milk

Break bread and soak in water for about 2 hours. Drain
and squeeze dry. Fry onions gently in dripping until
soft but not brown. Turn onions (and dripping) into
bread and mix well with herbs, suet and seasoning.
Beat egg in milk and stir into mixture. Turn into a well-
greased baking tin and cook in a moderate oven for 30
minutes.

141. Beetroot and Cheese Bake   *Serves 4*

1 lb (480 g) boiled
   beetroot, sliced
1 lb (480 g) boiled
   potatoes, sliced
2 tbsps chopped parsley
8 oz (240 g) onions,
   chopped

$\frac{1}{2}$ oz (15 g) dripping
$\frac{1}{2}$ oz (15 g) plain flour
$\frac{1}{4}$ pt (1 $\frac{1}{2}$ dl) milk
salt, pepper
2 oz (60 g) cheese,
   grated

Put layers of potatoes, parsley and beetroot into a well-greased pie dish. Repeat layers, finishing with potatoes. Fry onions gently in dripping until soft but not brown. Remove from heat and sprinkle in flour. Stir in milk and seasoning. Return to heat and cook until mixture thickens, then pour over beetroot mixture. Top with cheese and bake in a hot oven until brown (20 to 30 minutes).

142. Cabbage and Cheese Bake   *Serves 4*

1 medium cabbage,
   boiled
4 oz (120 g) cheese,
   grated
2 oz (60 g) breadcrumbs
cayenne pepper

white sauce (as recipe
   no. 305), using 1 oz
   (30 g) butter, 1 oz
   (30 g) flour and $\frac{1}{2}$ pt
   (3 dl) milk

Shred cabbage and place in a well-greased pie dish. Stir 2 oz (60 g) cheese and the breadcrumbs and pepper into the white sauce and pour over cabbage. Top with remaining cheese and bake in a hot oven until cheese is brown (15 to 20 minutes).

143. Cauliflower Hot Pot   *Serves 4*

1 small cauliflower (an
  old one with useless
  leaves is suitable)
2 oz (60 g) cheese,
  grated
2 tbsps chopped parsley
2 tbsps milk
cayenne pepper, salt

8 oz (240 g) tomatoes,
  sliced
8 oz (240 g) onions,
  grated
1 oz (30 g) butter
1 ½ lb (720 g) boiled
  potatoes

Boil cauliflower, strain, then mash to a creamy pulp.
Stir in cheese, parsley, 1 tablespoon milk and seasoning. Put a layer into a well-greased pie dish, followed
by layers of tomatoes and onions. Dot lightly with ½ oz
(15 g) butter, repeat layers and top with the potatoes
mashed with remaining milk and butter and more
seasoning. Bake in a hot oven until brown (20 to 30
minutes).

144. Cauliflower Pie   *Serves 4*

1 small cauliflower, in
  sprigs
1 ½ lb (720 g) potatoes
4 oz (120 g) cheese,
  grated
3 hardboiled eggs,
  sliced

¼ pt (1 ½ dl) sour milk
2 tbsps chopped parsley
cayenne pepper
celery salt
1 oz (30 g) breadcrumbs
a little butter

Boil cauliflower and potatoes separately, then drain.
When cool, slice potatoes and place a layer in a well-
greased pie dish, followed by layers of cauliflower,
cheese and eggs. Moisten with sour milk and sprinkle
parsley and seasoning over. Repeat layers, finishing
with potatoes. Top with breadcrumbs and dot with
butter. Bake in a hot oven until brown (20 to 30
minutes).

145. Ted and Daisy's Cauliflower Cheese Pudding

Serves 4

6 oz (180 g) cauliflower
   sprigs, boiled
4 oz (120 g) cheese,
   grated

2 oz (60 g) peas, boiled
2 oz (60 g) margarine
3 eggs, separated
salt, pepper

Mix together cauliflower sprigs and peas, then place in a well-greased pie dish. Cream together margarine and yolks of eggs, then stir in cheese and seasoning. Beat whites of eggs until stiff and fold into mixture, then pour over vegetables in pie dish. Bake in a moderately hot oven until golden brown (25 to 30 minutes).

146. French Bean and Egg Savoury

Serves 4

$1 \frac{1}{2}$ lb (720 g) French
   beans, sliced
3 hardboiled eggs,
   sliced
white sauce (as recipe
   no. 305), using 1 oz
   (30 g) butter,

1 oz (30 g) flour and
   $\frac{1}{2}$ pt (3 dl) milk
1 oz (30 g) cheese,
   grated
1 oz (30 g) breadcrumbs
a little butter

Boil beans until tender; drain and place a layer in a well-greased pie dish. Put a layer of eggs on top and repeat layers finishing with beans. Pour white sauce over and top with mixture of cheese and breadcrumbs. Dot with butter and bake in a hot oven for 20 minutes.

147. Fungus Soufflé   *Serves 4*

6 oz (180 g) mushrooms,
    puffballs,
    chanterelles or other
    edible fungi, cut
    small
2 oz (60 g) onions (or
    shallots), chopped
fat for frying

white sauce (as recipe
    no. 305), using $\frac{1}{2}$ oz
    (15 g) butter, $\frac{1}{2}$ oz
    (15 g) flour and $\frac{1}{4}$ pt
    (1 $\frac{1}{2}$ dl) milk
2 tbsps chopped parsley
salt, pepper
3 eggs, separated

Fry fungi and onions gently until tender. Remove from
heat and stir in all other ingredients except whites of
eggs. Beat whites of eggs until stiff and fold into mixture. Turn into a well-greased pie dish and bake in a
moderately hot oven for 20 minutes.

148. Jerusalem Artichoke Soufflé   *Serves 4*

1 lb (480 g) Jerusalem
    artichokes, diced
2 eggs, separated
$\frac{1}{4}$ pt (1 $\frac{1}{2}$ dl) milk
2 tbsps chopped parsley

salt, pepper
1 oz (30 g) butter
2 oz (60 g) breadcrumbs
2 oz (60 g) cheese,
    grated

Boil artichokes until cooked (about 20 minutes), strain
and mash. Stir in yolks of eggs, milk, parsley and seasoning. Beat egg whites until stiff and fold in. Grease a
pie dish with $\frac{1}{2}$ oz (15 g) butter and pour mixture in.
Top with mixture of breadcrumbs and cheese. Dot with
remaining butter and cook in a moderately hot oven
until brown (20 to 30 minutes).

149. Leek and Soya Savoury

Serves 4

4 oz (120 g) soyabean
   flour
1 lb (480 g) leeks, cut
   small
2 oz (60 g) cheese,
   grated

2 tbsps oatmeal
$\frac{1}{4}$ pt (1 $\frac{1}{2}$ dl) milk
$\frac{1}{2}$ tsp yeast extract
pepper

Boil leeks until tender, then strain—keeping $\frac{1}{4}$ pt (1 $\frac{1}{2}$ dl) liquor. Mix together soyabean flour, cheese and oatmeal and put a layer into a well-greased pie dish. Cover with half of the leeks, then repeat layers, finishing with soya mixture. Add milk to reserved leek liquor and stir in yeast extract and pepper. Pour into pie dish, then bake in a moderate oven for 1 hour.

150. Parsnip and Nut Soufflé

Serves 4

1 lb (480 g) parsnips, cut
   small
2 oz (60 g) nuts, chopped
1 oz (30 g) cheese,
   grated

2 oz (60 g) plain flour
grated nutmeg
salt
$\frac{1}{4}$ pt (1 $\frac{1}{2}$ dl) milk
2 eggs, separated

Boil parsnips until soft (about 20 minutes). Drain and mash to a pulp, then stir in all other ingredients except whites of eggs. Beat whites of eggs until stiff, then fold into mixture. Turn into a well-greased pie dish and bake in a moderate oven until golden-brown on top (about 25 minutes).

151. Pea and Tomato (September) Hot Pot *Serves 4*

12 oz (360 g) shelled
   peas from the last
   pickings, when they
   are a little tough
6 oz (180 g) tomatoes,
   sliced

3 hardboiled eggs,
   sliced
1 ½ lb (720 g) boiled
   potatoes, mashed
a little dripping
salt, pepper

Boil peas until tender (about 30 minutes), then strain.
Line a greased pie dish with potatoes. Put in a layer of
peas, then a layer of tomatoes and eggs sprinkled with
seasoning. Repeat layers and top with potatoes. Dot
with dripping and bake in a hot oven until brown (20 to
30 minutes).

152. Potato and Nut Soufflé *Serves 4*

2 oz (60 g) nuts, chopped
1 lb (480 g) potatoes
½ oz (15 g) butter
¼ pt (1 ½ dl) milk
2 eggs, separated

salt, pepper
1 oz (30 g) cheese,
   grated
a little grated nutmeg

Boil potatoes, then mash with all other ingredients
except whites of eggs, cheese and nutmeg. Beat whites
of eggs until stiff and fold into mixture, then turn into a
10 × 8 × 2-in (25 × 20 × 5-cm) greased baking tin.
Sprinkle with cheese and nutmeg, then bake in a hot
oven until crisp and brown (about 20 minutes).

153. Spinach and Cheese Savoury   Serves 4

2 lb (960 g) spinach
3 oz (90 g) cheese,
   grated

8 oz (240 g) onions,
   grated
salt, pepper

Boil freshly washed spinach (without water) for 5 to 10 minutes, until soft. Strain, chop and turn into a greased pie dish. Cover with onions, sprinkle seasoning over and top with cheese. Bake in a hot oven until cheese is brown (15 to 20 minutes).

154. Spinach and Lentils with Cheese   Serves 4

1 lb (480 g) spinach
6 oz (180 g) lentils
6 oz (180 g) tomatoes,
   sliced
salt, pepper

1 tbsp chopped fresh
   mint
3 oz (90 g) cheese,
   grated

Simmer lentils in about $\frac{3}{4}$ pt ($4\frac{1}{2}$ dl) water for about 20 minutes, stirring occasionally. (All water must be absorbed but it may be necessary to add some during cooking.) Simmer freshly washed spinach without water until cooked. Strain and place on bottom of a well-greased pie dish. Arrange tomatoes on top and sprinkle with seasoning and mint. Stir seasoning into lentils, then turn on to tomatoes and spinach. Smooth with fork and sprinkle cheese over. Bake in a hot oven until top is brown (about 30 minutes).

155. Tomato and Cheese Savoury   *Serves 4*

12 oz (360 g) tomatoes,
   sliced
4 oz (120 g) cheese,
   grated
12 oz (360 g) onions,
   chopped

$\frac{1}{4}$ pt (1 $\frac{1}{2}$ dl) milk
4 tbsps chopped parsley
salt, pepper
2 oz (60 g) breadcrumbs
a little butter

Simmer onion gently in milk until tender, then remove
from heat. Put tomatoes into a greased pie dish. Stir 3
oz (90 g) cheese, parsley and seasoning into the onions
and milk, then pour over tomatoes. Top with mixture of
breadcrumbs and remaining cheese. Dot with butter
and bake in a hot oven until brown (20 to 30 minutes).

156. Tomato and Haricot Bean Cheese Bake   *Serves 4*

8 oz (240 g) tomatoes,
   sliced
6 oz (180 g) haricot
   beans, soaked
   overnight
8 oz (240 g) onions,
   sliced

white sauce (as recipe
   no. 305), using 1 oz
   (30 g) butter, 1 oz
   (30 g) flour and $\frac{1}{4}$ pt
   (1 $\frac{1}{2}$ dl) milk
3 oz (90 g) cheese,
   grated
$\frac{1}{2}$ tsp dry mustard

Simmer beans and onions together until tender (about
1 $\frac{1}{2}$ hours). Strain and reserve $\frac{1}{4}$ pt (1 $\frac{1}{2}$ dl) of the liquor.
Stir reserved liquor into white sauce with 2 oz (60 g) of
cheese and the mustard. Return pan to heat and cook
gently until sauce thickens. Put beans and onion mixture into a well-greased pie dish, arrange tomatoes on
top, then pour over cheese sauce. Sprinkle remaining
cheese on top and bake in a hot oven until brown (20 to
30 minutes).

157. Turnip Pie

1 lb (480 g) turnips,
  sliced
4 oz (120 g) cheese,
  grated

4 oz (120 g)
  breadcrumbs
2 tbsps chopped chives
cayenne pepper, salt
$\frac{1}{2}$ pt (3 dl) milk

Boil turnips for 10 minutes, drain and turn into a well-greased pie dish. Mix 2 oz (60 g) of the cheese with the breadcrumbs, chives, seasoning and milk, and pour over turnips. Top with remaining cheese and cook in a hot oven until brown (20 to 30 minutes).

158. Turnip and Lentil Bake

8 oz (240 g) turnips (or
  swedes), grated
6 oz (180 g) lentils
$\frac{1}{2}$ tsp yeast extract
1 egg, beaten

2 oz (60 g) breadcrumbs
3 tbsps chopped parsley
pepper
1 $\frac{1}{2}$ oz (45 g) butter

Simmer lentils and turnips (or swedes) in about $\frac{3}{4}$ pt ($4\frac{1}{2}$ dl) water for about 20 minutes, stirring occasionally. (All water must be absorbed but it may be necessary to add some during cooking.) Stir in all other ingredients except a little of the butter. Turn into a well-greased pie dish, dot with remaining butter and bake in a hot oven until top is brown (about 30 minutes).

159. Vegetable Marrow and Butter Bean Bake

Serves 4

*half a medium
vegetable marrow
(cut lengthwise),
prepared and in one
piece*
3 oz (90 g) butter beans,
soaked overnight
5 oz (150 g) onions,
chopped
1 clove garlic, chopped

fat for frying
4 oz (120 g) tomatoes,
chopped
2 oz (60 g) cheese,
grated
2 tbsps chopped parsley
1 tsp mixed dried herbs
salt, pepper
a little butter

Simmer butter beans until soft (about 2 hours) then
strain. Lay marrow (hollow uppermost) in a well-
greased baking tin. Fry onions and garlic gently until
soft but not brown. Add tomatoes and continue cooking
for 5 minutes, then mix with all other ingredients
except marrow and butter. Fork mixture into hollow of
marrow, dot with butter and bake in a moderate oven
until marrow is soft (45 minutes to 1 hour).

160. Butter Bean Roast

Serves 4

6 oz (180 g) butter
beans, soaked
overnight
4 oz (120 g) onions,
chopped
1 clove garlic, chopped
fat for frying

8 oz (240 g) tomatoes,
chopped
3 oz (90 g) breadcrumbs
4 tbsps chopped parsley
1 tbsp Worcestershire
sauce
salt, pepper
a little butter

Simmer butter beans until soft (about 2 hours), then
drain and mash. Fry onions and garlic gently until soft
but not brown, then mix together all ingredients except
butter. Turn into a well-greased 1-lb (or 500-g) loaf tin,
dot with butter, cover with foil and cook in a moderate
oven for 1 hour.

161. Dried Pea and Cheese Pie

Serves 4

6 oz (180 g) dried peas,
   soaked overnight
4 oz (120 g) cheese,
   grated
1 oz (30 g) butter
8 oz (240 g) onions,
   sliced

4 tbsps breadcrumbs
2 eggs, beaten
1 tbsp chutney
1 ½ lb (720 g) boiled
   potatoes, mashed
4 tbsps chopped chives
cayenne pepper, salt

Simmer peas until soft (about 1 hour). Melt butter in a saucepan, and fry onions gently for 5 minutes. Mix together peas, onions, breadcrumbs, egg and chutney and turn into a greased pie dish. Mix potatoes, chives and seasoning and fork into the pie dish. Sprinkle cheese over and bake in a hot oven until brown on top (20 to 30 minutes).

162. Lentil Roast

Serves 4

6 oz (180 g) lentils
1 oz (30 g) dripping
6 oz (180 g) carrots,
   grated
2 oz (60 g) oatmeal

1 egg, beaten
2 tbsps chopped fresh
   mint
1 clove garlic, chopped
salt, pepper

Simmer lentils in about ½ pt (3 dl) water for about 20 minutes, stirring occasionally. (All water must be absorbed but it may be necessary to add some during cooking.) Stir in dripping, then all other ingredients. Turn into a well-greased 1-lb (or 500-g) loaf tin, cover with foil and cook in a moderate oven for 1 hour.

163. Lentil and Walnut Roast   *Serves 4*

6 oz (180 g) lentils
4 oz (120 g) walnuts,
    chopped
8 oz (240 g) onions,
    chopped
1 clove garlic, chopped
fat for frying

3 oz (90 g) breadcrumbs
1 egg, beaten
4 tbsps chopped parsley
1 tbsp tomato sauce
1 tsp mixed dried herbs
salt, pepper

Simmer lentils in about $\frac{1}{2}$ pt (3 dl) water for about 20
minutes, stirring occasionally. (All water must be
absorbed but it may be necessary to add some during
cooking.) Fry onions and garlic gently until soft but not
brown, then mix together all ingredients. Turn into a
well-greased 1-lb (or 500-g) loaf tin, cover with foil and
cook in a moderate oven for 1 hour.

164. Lentil Savoury   *Serves 4*

6 oz (180 g) lentils
8 oz (240 g) onions,
    chopped
1 lb (480 g) boiled
    potatoes, mashed

4 tbsps chopped parsley
1 tbsp chutney
salt, pepper
a little butter

Simmer lentils and onions in about $\frac{3}{4}$ pt ($4\frac{1}{2}$ dl) water for
about 20 minutes, stirring occasionally. (All water
must be absorbed, but it may be necessary to add some
during cooking.) Stir in all other ingredients except
butter, then turn into a well-greased, oven-proof dish.
Dot with butter and cook in a hot oven until brown on
top (about 20 minutes).

165. Lentil and Cheese Pie   *Serves 4*

6 oz (180 g) lentils
3 oz (90 g) cheese,
  grated
6 oz (180 g) onions,
  grated
2 tbsps chopped parsley

1 tsp mixed dried herbs
$\frac{1}{2}$ tsp yeast extract
pepper
grated nutmeg
1 oz (30 g) breadcrumbs
a little butter

Simmer lentils in about $\frac{1}{2}$ pt (3 dl) water for about 20 minutes, stirring occasionally. (All water must be absorbed but it may be necessary to add some during cooking.) Then mix with 2 oz (60 g) cheese, the onions, parsley, herbs, yeast extract and pepper. Turn into a well-greased pie dish and sprinkle with nutmeg. Mix together the breadcrumbs and remaining cheese and spread on top. Dot with butter and bake in a hot oven until crisp and brown (20 to 30 minutes).

166. Nut Roast   *Serves 4*

8 oz (240 g) mixed nuts,
  chopped
6 oz (180 g)
  breadcrumbs
6 oz (180 g) onions,
  grated

2 oz (60 g) butter,
  melted
2 tbsps chopped parsley
$\frac{1}{2}$ tsp mixed dried herbs
1 tsp yeast extract
  dissolved in $\frac{1}{4}$ pt
  (1 $\frac{1}{2}$ dl) hot water

Mix together all ingredients and turn into a well-greased 1-lb (or 500-g) loaf tin. Cover with foil and cook in a moderate oven for 45 minutes.

167. Rice and Cheese Savoury   Serves 4

6 oz (180 g) rice
6 oz (180 g) cheese,
    grated
4 tbsps chopped chives
1 tsp baking powder

cayenne pepper, salt
1 egg
4 oz (120 g) plain flour
½ pt (3 dl) milk

Boil rice for 20 minutes, then drain. Beat egg well,
gradually adding flour and milk. Mix all ingredients
together, turn into a greased pie dish and bake in a
moderately hot oven for 30 minutes.

168. Egg and Cheese Pie (Wyau Mynydd)   Serves 4

4 hardboiled eggs, cut
    in two
4 oz (120 g) cheese,
    grated
1 lb (480 g) potatoes
12 oz (360 g) onions or
    leeks
½ oz (15 g) butter

2 tbsps chopped parsley
salt, pepper
white sauce (as recipe
    no. 305), using 1 oz
    (30 g) butter, 1 oz
    (30 g) flour and ¼ pt
    (1 ½ dl) milk

Boil potatoes and onions or leeks together until cooked,
then mash with butter, parsley and seasoning. Spread
mixture around sides of a well-greased pie dish and
arrange eggs on the bottom. Mix 2 oz (60 g) cheese with
the white sauce and pour over. Sprinkle remaining
cheese on top and bake in a hot oven until top is brown
(20 to 30 minutes).

169. Bread and Cheese Pudding   Serves 4

4 thick slices of bread
   and butter
4 oz (120 g) cheese,
   grated
½ tsp dry mustard

cayenne pepper
a little grated nutmeg
1 egg, beaten
¾ pt (4½ dl) milk
2 tbsps chopped chives

Place 2 slices of bread and butter (butter on top) in a
well-greased pie dish. Cover with 2 oz (60 g) cheese and
sprinkle mustard, cayenne pepper and nutmeg over.
Place the other two slices of bread and butter on top
(buttered side up). Beat egg with milk and pour over
bread and butter. Cover with remaining cheese and
sprinkle more mustard, cayenne pepper and nutmeg
over. Top with chives and leave to stand for 25
minutes. Cook in a moderate oven for 30 minutes.

170. Cheese Pudding (Pwdin Caws)   Serves 4

4 oz (120 g) cheese,
   grated
5 oz (150 g)
   breadcrumbs
½ pt (3 dl) milk

2 eggs, separated
4 tbsps chopped chives
1 tsp dry mustard
cayenne pepper

Put breadcrumbs into bowl, pour milk over and soak
for 10 minutes. Add all other ingredients except whites
of eggs and mix thoroughly. Whisk whites of eggs until
stiff, then fold into mixture. Turn into a well-greased
pie dish and cook in a moderately hot oven until brown
(20 to 30 minutes).

171. Bread and Cheese Soufflé   Serves 4

2 $\frac{1}{2}$ oz (75 g) $\frac{1}{4}$ pt (1 $\frac{1}{2}$ dl) milk
  breadcrumbs   2 tbsps chopped chives
2 $\frac{1}{2}$ oz (75 g) cheese,   cayenne pepper
  grated   2 eggs, separated
1 oz (30 g) butter

Melt butter in saucepan, then stir in all other ingredients except whites of eggs. Beat whites of eggs until
stiff and fold into mixture. Turn into a well-greased pie
dish and bake in a moderate oven for 30 minutes.

172. Poor Man's Cheese Soufflé   Serves 4

2 oz (60 g) cheese, $\frac{1}{4}$ pt (1 $\frac{1}{2}$ dl) milk
  grated   cayenne pepper
1 oz (30 g) butter   1 egg, separated
1 oz (30 g) plain flour

Melt butter in saucepan, blend in flour, slowly add milk
whilst stirring over a very low heat. Then stir in
cheese, cayenne pepper and yolk of egg. Remove from
heat. Beat white of egg until stiff, then fold into mixture. Turn into a well-greased pie dish and bake in a
hot oven for 20 minutes.

173. Cheese and Butter Bean Flan   Serves 4

4 oz (120 g) cheese,
   grated
4 oz (120 g) butter
   beans, soaked
   overnight
plain pastry (as recipe
   no. 295), using 2 oz
   (60 g) margarine and
   5 oz (150 g) flour

8 oz (240 g) onions,
   sliced
fat for frying
1 tsp dry mustard
2 eggs, beaten
$\frac{1}{4}$ pt (1 $\frac{1}{2}$ dl) milk
2 tbsps chopped parsley
salt, pepper

Simmer butter beans until soft (about 2 hours) then
drain. Line an 8–9-in (20–22$\frac{1}{2}$-cm) flan tin with the
pastry. Fry the onions gently until soft but not brown,
then turn into flan case. Put butter beans on top, cover
with cheese and sprinkle mustard over. Beat eggs with
milk, parsley and seasoning, then pour over flan. Bake
in a hot oven for 10 minutes, then in a slow oven for 30
minutes.

174. Cheese and Carrot Flan   Serves 4

4 oz (120 g) cheese,
   grated
6 oz (180 g) carrots,
   grated
plain pastry (as recipe
   no. 295), using

2 oz (60 g) margarine
   and 5 oz (150 g) flour
2 eggs, beaten
$\frac{1}{4}$ pt (1 $\frac{1}{2}$ dl) milk
2 tbsps chopped chives
salt, pepper

Line an 8–9-in (20–22$\frac{1}{2}$-cm) flan tin with the pastry.
Beat eggs with milk and stir in all other ingredients.
Turn into flan case and bake in a moderately hot oven
for 5 minutes then in a slow oven for 1 hour.

175. Cheese and Onion Flan (1)   Serves 4

4 oz (120 g) cheese,
   grated
5 oz (150 g) onions,
   grated
plain pastry (as recipe
   no. 295), using 2 oz
   (60 g) margarine and
   5 oz (150 g) flour

4 oz (120 g) tomatoes,
   chopped
2 eggs, beaten
$\frac{1}{4}$ pt (1 $\frac{1}{2}$ dl) milk
2 tbsps chopped parsley
cayenne pepper, salt

Line an 8–9-in (20–22$\frac{1}{2}$-cm) flan tin with the pastry,
then arrange onions and tomatoes in it and sprinkle
cheese over. Beat eggs in milk with parsley and
cayenne pepper. Pour over flan mixture and bake in a
moderately hot oven for 5 minutes, then in a slow oven
for 1 hour.

176. Cheese and Onion Flan (2)   Serves 4

3 oz (90 g) cheese,
   grated
8 oz (240 g) onions,
   sliced
plain pastry (as recipe
   no. 295), using 2 oz
   (60 g) margarine and
   5 oz (150 g) flour
fat for frying

2 tbsps chopped parsley
white sauce (as recipe
   no. 305), using 1 oz
   (30 g) butter, 1 oz
   (30 g) flour and $\frac{1}{2}$ pt
   (3 dl) milk
4 oz (120 g) tomatoes,
   sliced

Line an 8–9-in (20–22$\frac{1}{2}$-cm) flan tin with the pastry.
Fry the onions gently until soft and slightly browned.
Stir parsley and 2 oz (60 g) cheese into the white sauce.
Mix tomatoes with onion and turn into flan case then
pour white sauce over. Sprinkle remaining cheese on
top and bake in a moderately hot oven for 30 minutes.

177. Cheese and Egg Pasties

Makes 2

4 oz (120 g) cheese,
   grated
3 eggs, beaten
plain pastry (as recipe
   no. 295), using 3 oz
   (90 g) fat and
   8 oz (240 g) flour

1 oz (30 g) butter
1 tsp Worcestershire
   sauce
salt, pepper
a little milk

Divide pastry into two and roll each piece into a circle.
Melt butter in a saucepan then stir in cheese, eggs,
Worcestershire sauce and seasoning. Heat gently until
mixture thickens, then spoon half of mixture on to each
pastry round. Draw up opposite sides of pastry,
moisten edges and press together, fluting with the
fingers. Brush with milk, prick both sides with a fork
and bake in a hot oven for 5 minutes, then in a
moderate oven for 10 minutes.

178. Cheese and Onion Pasties

Makes 2

3 oz (90 g) cheese,
   grated
8 oz (240 g) onions,
   grated
plain pastry (as recipe

no. 295), using 3 oz
   (90 g) fat and 8 oz
   (240 g) flour
salt, pepper
a little milk

Divide pastry into two and roll each piece into a circle.
Mix together cheese, onion and seasoning. Put half of
the mixture on each pastry round. Draw up opposite
sides of pastry, moisten edges and press together,
fluting with the fingers. Brush with milk, prick both
sides with a fork and bake in a hot oven for 10 minutes,
then in a moderate oven for 15 minutes.

179. Vegetable Pie with Cheese Pastry   Serves 4

1 ½ lb (720 g) mixed root
   vegetables, diced
4 oz (120 g) onions,
   sliced
1 clove garlic, chopped
1 small can baked
   beans
4 tbsps chopped parsley

salt, pepper
plain pastry (as recipe
   no. 295), using 4 oz
   (120 g) flour, 1 oz
   (30 g) oatmeal, 1 oz
   (30 g) fat and 2 oz
   (60 g) cheese, grated
a little milk

Simmer together all vegetables until cooked. Strain
(saving the liquor), add seasoning and mix with baked
beans. Turn into a well-greased pie dish and sprinkle
with parsley. Cover with pastry lid. Brush with milk,
make a slit in top and bake in a moderate oven until
brown (30 to 40 minutes).

Do not discard the vegetable liquor. If you have
boiled the vegetables without salt (and you *should*
have) the saved liquor makes a delicious gravy or
pre-dinner drink. In this particular recipe I consider
that no gravy is needed with the pie, so why not drink
the vegetable liquor flavoured with ¼ teaspoon yeast
extract?

5. Puddings

180. Strawberry Pudding
181. Blackberry Pudding
182. Date Pudding
183. Fig Pudding
184. Treacle Pudding
185. Chocolate Coconut Pudding
186. Apple and Lemon Pudding
187. Mincemeat Pudding
188. Demerara Pudding
189. Raspberry Roll
190. Currant Roll
191. Jam Roll
192. Treacle Roll
193. Treacle Tart
194. Date and Treacle Tart
195. Lemon Crust Tart
196. Hafod Apple Tart
197. Rhubarb Tart (1)
198. Rhubarb Tart (2)
199. Chocolate Flan
200. Carrot Chocolate Flan
201. Lemon Curd Flan
202. Apple and Lemon Flan
203. Apple Bake
204. Apple Economy Pie
205. Apple and Breadcrumb Pie
206. Apple Batter
207. Apple Crunch
208. Bread and Butter Pudding
209. Bread and Marmalade Pudding
210. Bread and Plum Pudding
211. Bread and Rhubarb Pudding
212. Chocolate Bread Pudding
213. Date and Rice Pudding
214. Banana Custard Bake
215. Rhubarb Gingerbread Pudding
216. Queen of Raspberry Puddings
217. Jam Sponge Pudding
218. Lemon Soufflé

'What shall we have for pudding?' is a question easily answered by the housewife who has fruit growing in the garden. The heavenly aroma of blackcurrant tart sets my mouth watering even just to think of it. The exquisite flavour of elderflower-flavoured stewed gooseberries ... the delight in a bowl of fresh raspberries topped with cream ... a few strawberries upon your breakfast cereal ... these are some of the pleasures for those who grow fruit in their garden. Fruit plants need not take up much room; they don't involve very much work and, anyway, the rewards at fruit-gathering time make it all worthwhile.

At Hafod we ate fresh fruit daily in the summer and, of course, I bottled some and made jam for my winter stores. I think my favourite tart was one made from mixed fruit, containing all the odds and ends in between the seasons; the last few strawberries and blackcurrants would be mixed with the first of the gooseberries and raspberries—a combination of sweetly sharp flavours that has no equal.

In the cold days of early spring, when my stores of bottled fruit were running low, I made treacle puddings, or spicy currant rolls, or puddings of chocolate and coconut, coated with a smooth, rich chocolate sauce. But for a tasty and satisfying pudding of sheer unbeatable economy, I recommend 'Brown Betty' (recipe no. 188). Nutritionists may boggle at the ingredients (it consists of nothing but spiced flour, suet and sugar), and the first time I tried it I did so with extreme doubt. I didn't think it would work. All those carbohydrates tied up in a rag! It sounded most indigestible. But it wasn't. The demerara sugar becomes a toffee-like treacly ooze inside the spicy softness of the surrounding dough. The flavour is something between butterscotch and caramel and suggests all sorts of nice fruity things so that you can hardly believe that it is not stuffed with apricots or oranges. But it isn't. It is just spiced flour, suet and sugar and I recommend you to serve it with Butterscotch Sauce (recipe no. 310). This is another recipe where the delicious final result belies the cheap ingredients involved.

There are several sweet sauces in the Miscellaneous section, any of which will combine well with some of the plainer suet puddings, but I must admit to a liking for vanilla custard sauce. This liking dates back to my childhood. Although, as a special treat, my mother sometimes baked deliciously-nutmeggy egg-custards, our normal every-day custard sauce came out of a packet. When she was serving up stewed fruit and custard (and with a garden producing large quantities of rhubarb, apples and pears this happened fairly frequently) she allowed me to take my fruit and my custard in two separate dishes. In a household not given to catering for childish fads, this was surprising—and in case you are thinking that my fussiness was an early indication of a fastidious and discriminating palate that objected to the purity of the fruit being contaminated by the synthetics in the custard powder, I must disillusion you. I wanted to get rid of the fruit as quickly as possible in order that I might linger lovingly over the warm and cloying smoothness of the custard.

Custard powder must be one of the most popular and longest-standing convenience foods on the market. I have a carton of it in my cupboard right now . . . and I wouldn't mind betting that you have too. I know that it is just so much cornflour, chemical flavouring and dye, and I can't rid myself of that twinge of guilt each time I buy some—but my depraved childhood taste remains. I like the stuff.

Real custard, of course, consists of nothing but eggs, milk and sugar, flavoured perhaps with a little nutmeg or cinnamon. It is delicious and nourishing, but it is more expensive and needs slow and careful cooking. No wonder that the woman in a hurry grabs a packet of powder instead.

However, as a compromise, allow me to offer you recipe no. 311. This was given to me recently by a friend who is always in a hurry, but also refuses to feed her family on rubbish. Sandra's custard can be lightly flavoured in any way you wish, and I now use it any time I want a custard sauce—if I can spare an egg. And if I can't . . . well, there is still that carton of powder left in the cupboard!

180. Strawberry Pudding

Serves 4–6

8 oz (240 g)
 strawberries, halved
2 oz (60 g) butter
2 oz (60 g) sugar

1 egg, beaten
4 oz (120 g) self-raising
 flour
2 tbsps milk

Cream together butter and sugar, then add the egg, flour and milk. Beat thoroughly, then stir in strawberries. Turn into a well-greased 2-pt (12-dl) pudding basin, cover and boil for $2\frac{1}{2}$ hours.

181. Blackberry Pudding

Serves 4–6

8 oz (240 g) blackberry
 jam
4 oz (120 g) self-raising
 flour

3 oz (90 g) suet
2 oz (60 g) breadcrumbs
1 oz (30 g) sugar
a little milk

Mix together flour, suet, breadcrumbs and sugar. Add milk to make soft dough, and stir in blackberry jam. Mix all together thoroughly. Turn mixture into a well-greased 2-pt (12-dl) pudding basin, cover and boil for $2\frac{1}{2}$ hours.

182. Date Pudding

Serves 4–6

6 oz (180 g) dates, chopped

4 oz (120 g) breadcrumbs

3 oz (90 g) suet

2 oz (60 g) self-raising flour

1 oz (30 g) sugar

$\frac{1}{2}$ tsp cinnamon

1 egg, beaten

$\frac{1}{4}$ pt (1 $\frac{1}{2}$ dl) milk

Mix together all dry ingredients, then add egg beaten with milk. Mix thoroughly, then turn into a well-greased 2-pt (12-dl) pudding basin. Cover and boil for $2\frac{1}{2}$ hours.

183. Fig Pudding

Serves 4–6

4 oz (120 g) dried figs, chopped

$\frac{1}{4}$ pt (1 $\frac{1}{2}$ dl) sour milk

6 oz (180 g) plain flour

3 oz (90 g) suet

1 tsp mixed spice

1 tsp ground ginger

1 tsp bicarbonate of soda

2 tbsps black treacle

Mix together all dry ingredients, then beat in milk and treacle. Turn into a well-greased 2-pt (12-dl) pudding basin, cover and boil for $2\frac{1}{2}$ hours. Serve with Butterscotch Sauce (recipe no. 310).

184. Treacle Pudding
Serves 4–6

3 tbsps golden syrup
8 oz (240 g) self-raising
　flour
4 oz (120 g) suet

4 oz (120 g) brown sugar
1 lemon
milk to mix

Mix together flour, suet and sugar. Stir in grated rind of lemon and half the juice, then add milk to make soft dough. Spoon golden syrup into a well-greased 2-pt (12-dl) pudding basin, then add remaining lemon juice. Turn dough into basin. Cover and boil for $2\frac{1}{2}$ hours.

VARIATIONS
Omit golden syrup and lemon and mix in 6 oz (180 g) mixed dried fruit and 1 tsp mixed spice.

OR
Omit golden syrup and lemon and mix in 2 tbsps cocoa, 4 oz (120 g) dates, chopped, and 2 oz (60 g) nuts, chopped. Serve with hot Chocolate Sauce (as variation of recipe no. 311).

OR
Omit golden syrup, lemon and milk, and use juice from 1 small can of fruit to mix dough. Place fruit with remaining juice in a well-greased 2-pt (12-dl) pudding basin and cover with dough as in basic recipe.

185. Chocolate Coconut Pudding
Serves 4–6

2 tbsps cocoa
2 oz (60 g) desiccated
　coconut
3 oz (90 g) margarine
2 oz (60 g) sugar

1 egg, beaten
6 oz (180 g) self-raising
　flour
1 tbsp milk

Cream together margarine and sugar, add cocoa and egg and mix thoroughly, then beat in flour, milk and coconut. Turn into a well-greased 2-pt (12-dl) pudding basin. Cover and boil for $2\frac{1}{2}$ hours. Serve with hot Chocolate Sauce (as variation of recipe no. 311).

186. Apple and Lemon Pudding

Serves 4 – 6

8 oz (240 g) cooking
  apples, chopped
1 lemon
2 oz (60 g) sultanas
2 oz (60 g) breadcrumbs
1 tbsp golden syrup

For the pastry
4 oz (120 g) suet
8 oz (240 g) self-raising
  flour

Mix together flour and suet, then add water to make stiff dough. Roll and cut into rounds to make layers in a 2-pt (12-dl) pudding basin. Mix juice and grated rind of lemon with rest of ingredients. Place round of pastry in greased pudding basin and cover with a layer of the mixture. Repeat layers, finishing with pastry. Cover and boil for $2\frac{1}{2}$ hours.

187. Mincemeat Pudding

Serves 4 – 6

1 lb (480 g) mincemeat

For the pastry
4 oz (120 g) suet
8 oz (240 g) self-raising
  flour

Mix together flour and suet, then add water to make stiff dough. Roll and cut into rounds to make layers in a 2-pt (12-dl) pudding basin. Place a round of pastry in greased pudding basin and cover with a layer of mincemeat. Repeat layers finishing with pastry. Cover and boil for $2\frac{1}{2}$ hours.

188. Demerara Pudding (Brown Betty)   Serves 4 – 6

4 oz (120 g) demerara
  sugar
8 oz (240 g) self-raising
  flour

4 oz (120 g) suet
1 tsp mixed spice

Mix together flour, suet and spice. Add water to make soft dough, then roll into an oblong and moisten edges. Sprinkle sugar over, then roll up and seal edges. Tie in a cloth, lower into boiling water and simmer for 2 hours. Serve with Butterscotch Sauce (recipe no. 310).

189. Raspberry Roll   Serves 4 – 6

12 oz (360 g)
  raspberries
8 oz (240 g) self-raising
  flour

4 oz (120 g) suet
2 oz (60 g) white sugar
2 oz (60 g) demerara
  sugar

Mix together flour, suet and white sugar, then add water to make soft dough. Roll into oblong and moisten edges. Sprinkle demerara sugar over and cover with raspberries, then roll up and seal edges. Tie in a cloth, lower into boiling water and simmer for 2 hours.

190. Currant Roll (Spotted Dick)   Serves 4 – 6

4 oz (120 g) currants
6 oz (180 g) self-raising
  flour
4 oz (120 g) suet
2 oz (60 g) breadcrumbs

2 oz (60 g) Barbados
  sugar
1 tsp mixed spice
milk to mix

Mix together all dry ingredients. Add milk to make soft dough, then form into a roll. Tie in a cloth, lower into boiling water and simmer for 2 hours. Serve with a generous sprinkle of Barbados sugar.

191. Jam Roll (baked or boiled)   *Serves 4 – 6*

8 oz (240 g) jam   For the pastry
a little milk and sugar   *4 oz (120 g) suet*
(if baking)   *8 oz (240 g) self-raising*
                                      flour

Mix together flour and suet, then add water to make
soft dough. Roll into an oblong and moisten edges.
Spread jam over, then roll up and seal edges.
If baking: Brush with milk and sprinkle with sugar.
Cook in a moderate oven for 30 minutes.
If boiling: Tie in a cloth, lower into boiling water and
simmer for $1\frac{1}{2}$ hours.

192. Treacle Roll   *Serves 4 – 6*

4 tbsps golden syrup   *$\frac{1}{4}$ tsp salt*
8 oz (240 g) self-raising   *$\frac{3}{4}$ pt ($4\frac{1}{2}$ dl) milk*
flour   *(approx.)*
4 oz (120 g) suet

Mix together flour, suet and salt, then add water to
make soft dough. Roll into an oblong and moisten edges.
Spread golden syrup over, then roll up, seal edges and
place in a well-greased pie dish. Bring milk to the boil
and pour over roll. Cook in a moderate oven (basting
occasionally) for $1\frac{1}{2}$ hours.

193. Treacle Tart   *Serves 4 – 6*

4 tbsps golden syrup   For the pastry
2 oz (60 g) breadcrumbs   *3 oz (90 g) margarine*
1 lemon   *6 oz (180 g) plain flour*

Rub margarine into flour and add water to make soft
dough. Roll thinly and line a 10-in (25-cm) tart plate.
Sprinkle breadcrumbs over and add juice and grated
rind of lemon. Top with golden syrup and bake in a
moderate oven for 20 to 30 minutes. Leave until cold
before cutting.

194. Date and Treacle Tart

Serves 4 – 6

3 oz (90 g) dates,
  chopped
1 tbsp golden syrup
2 tbsps rolled (porridge)
  oats
a little margarine

For the pastry
2 oz (60 g) margarine
6 oz (180 g) plain flour
1 oz (30 g) sugar
a little milk

Rub margarine into flour and add sugar and enough milk to make soft dough. Roll out and line a 10-in (25-cm) tart plate. Cover with dates, then spread golden syrup and rolled oats over. Dot with margarine and cook in a moderate oven for 25 minutes. This can be eaten hot or cold.

195. Lemon Crust Tart

Serves 4 – 6

1 large lemon
1 egg, beaten
3 oz (90 g) sugar

For the pastry
3 oz (90 g) butter
6 oz (180 g) self-raising
  flour
a little milk and extra
  sugar

Rub butter into flour and add water to make stiff dough. Divide in two and roll each piece to fit a 10-in (25-cm) tart plate. Line the plate with half the pastry. Beat egg with sugar and juice and grated rind of lemon, then pour onto pastry-lined plate. Moisten edges, cover with other piece of pastry and fork edges together. Brush with milk, sprinkle sugar over and bake in a moderately hot oven until golden brown (about 25 minutes). Serve with Lemon Sauce (recipe no. 309).

196. Hafod Apple Tart

Serves 4–6

1 lb (480 g) cooking
   apples, sliced
¼ tsp ground cloves
2 oz (60 g) currants
3 tbsps breadcrumbs
3 tbsps golden syrup

For the pastry
2 oz (60 g) margarine
4 oz (120 g) plain flour
4 oz (120 g) oatmeal

Simmer apples with cloves in a little water until soft.
Rub margarine into flour and oatmeal and add water to
make stiff dough. Roll and line a 10 × 8 × 2-in (25 × 20
× 5-cm) baking tin. Mix currants with apples and turn
into pastry. Sprinkle with breadcrumbs and top with
golden syrup. Bake in a moderate oven for 30 minutes.

197. Rhubarb Tart (1) (Teisen Rhubarb)

Serves 4–6

8 oz (240 g) stewed
   rhubarb
a little milk and extra
   sugar

For the pastry
2 oz (60 g) margarine
6 oz (180 g) plain flour
1 oz (30 g) sugar
1 tsp baking powder
½ tsp mixed spice
1 egg, beaten

Rub margarine into flour then mix with other dry ingredients. Add egg and mix to form a very stiff and
crumbly dough. Divide in two and roll each piece to an
oblong. Put one half in a well-greased baking tin or
Swiss roll tin and cover with rhubarb, then top with
other half of pastry. Brush over with milk and sprinkle
with sugar. Bake in a moderately hot oven until golden-
brown (20 to 30 minutes). Leave until cold before
cutting.

198. Rhubarb Tart (2) (Teisen Rhubarb)   *Serves 4 – 6*

12 oz [360 g] rhubarb,
   cut into small pieces
4 oz [120 g] raisins
3 oz [90 g] sugar
$\frac{1}{2}$ oz [15 g] butter

For the pastry
4 oz [120 g] margarine
8 oz [240 g] self-raising
   flour
1 oz [30 g] sugar
a little milk and extra
   sugar

Simmer together rhubarb, raisins, sugar and butter gently until soft. Beat well and put aside to cool. Rub margarine into flour, add sugar, then enough water to make stiff dough. Divide in two and roll each piece to an oblong. Put one half in a well-greased 10 × 8 × 2-in (25 × 20 × 5-cm) baking tin, cover with the rhubarb mixture, and top with other half of pastry. Brush over with milk and sprinkle with sugar. Bake in a moderately hot oven until golden-brown (20 to 30 minutes).

199. Chocolate Flan   *Serves 4 – 6*

2 tbsps cocoa
3 oz [90 g] breadcrumbs
1 oz [30 g] sugar
4 tbsps milk
1 egg, beaten
a few drops vanilla
  essence

For the pastry
3 oz [90 g] margarine
6 oz [180 g] plain flour
a little milk

Rub margarine into flour and add milk to make stiff dough. Roll pastry and line an 8–9-in (20–20$\frac{1}{2}$-cm) flan tin (or tart plate). Mix together breadcrumbs, cocoa and sugar in a saucepan. Beat milk into egg, then pour over breadcrumb mixture. Add vanilla essence and cook gently, stirring continuously, for 10 minutes. Turn mixture into pastry case and bake in a moderate oven for 25 minutes.

200. Carrot Chocolate Flan (Air-Raid Tart) Serves 4 – 6

6 oz (180 g) boiled
   carrots, mashed
2 tbsps cocoa
2 oz (60 g) sugar
½ tsp vanilla essence

For the pastry
3 oz (90 g) margarine
6 oz (180 g) plain flour

Rub margarine into flour and add water to make stiff dough. Roll pastry and line an 8 – 9-in (20 – 20½-cm) flan tin (or tart plate). Mix together all other ingredients and turn into pastry case. Cook in a moderate oven for 30 minutes. Serve with Chocolate Sauce (as variation of recipe no. 311).

201. Lemon Curd Flan   Serves 4 – 6

5 or 6 tbsps lemon curd
   (see recipe no. 285)
½ pt (3 dl) thick
   custard

For the pastry
4 oz (120 g) butter
8 oz (240 g) plain flour

Rub butter into flour and add water to make soft dough. Roll pastry and line an 8 – 9-in (20 – 20½-cm) flan tin (or tart plate). Prick all over with fork and bake for 20 minutes in a moderate oven. Allow to cool, then spoon lemon curd in and cover with custard.

202. Apple and Lemon Flan   Serves 4 – 6

8 oz (240 g) cooking
   apples, grated
1 lemon
1 oz (30 g) butter
2 oz (60 g) sugar
1 egg, beaten

For the pastry
3 oz (90 g) margarine
6 oz (180 g) plain flour

Rub margarine into flour and add water to make stiff dough. Roll pastry and line an 8 – 9-in (20 – 22½-cm) flan tin (or tart plate). Cream butter and sugar together, then mix well with juice and grated rind of lemon, apples and egg. Turn into pastry case and bake in a moderate oven for 30 minutes.

203. Apple Bake

Serves 4 – 6

1 lb (480 g) cooking
   apples, grated
2 oz (60 g) sugar
4 oz (120 g) margarine

½ tsp ground cloves
1 egg, beaten
8 oz (240 g) self-raising
   flour

Cream together sugar and margarine, then add apples, ground cloves and egg. Beat well, gradually adding flour. Turn into a well-greased 10 × 8 × 2-in (25 × 20 × 5-cm) baking tin and cook in a moderate oven for 30 minutes.

204. Apple Economy Pie

Serves 4 – 6

8 oz (240 g) cooking
   apples, cut small
1 lb (480 g) marrow, cut
   small
2 oz (60 g) raisins
2 oz (60 g) demerara
   sugar
½ tsp mixed spice
half lemon

For the pastry
3 oz (90 g) margarine
6 oz (180 g) self-raising
   flour
a little milk and sugar

Mix together apples, marrow, raisins, demerara sugar, spice and grated rind of half lemon. Put mixture into a well-greased pie dish and squeeze lemon juice over. Rub margarine into flour and add water to make soft dough. Roll and fit pastry to pie dish in the form of a lid. Brush with milk then sprinkle with sugar. Cut slit in top and bake in a moderate oven for 1 hour. Serve with hot cornflour custard flavoured with juice from the remaining half lemon.

205. Apple and Breadcrumb Pie (Friar's Omelette)

Serves 4 – 6

1 lb (480 g) cooking
   apples, sliced
3 oz (90 g) breadcrumbs

2 oz (60 g) sugar
1 oz (30 g) butter
1 egg, beaten

Simmer apples until soft, mash, then stir in sugar, butter and egg. Mix well together. Put half the breadcrumbs to the bottom and sides of a well-greased pie dish. Turn mixture into pie dish and cover with remaining breadcrumbs. Bake for 30 minutes in a moderate oven.

206. Apple Batter

Serves 4 – 6

8 oz (240 g) cooking
   apples, grated
1 egg, beaten

$\frac{1}{2}$ pt (3 dl) milk
4 oz (120 g) self-raising
   flour
1 oz (30 g) dripping

Beat egg with milk, gradually adding flour, then stir in apples. Melt dripping in a 10 × 8 × 2-in (25 × 20 × 5-cm) baking tin and when hot pour in apple batter. Cook in a hot oven for 20 minutes. Serve sprinkled with lemon juice and sugar.

207. Apple Crunch

Serves 4 – 6

12 oz (360 g) cooking
   apples, sliced
1 oz (30 g) sultanas
$\frac{1}{2}$ tsp mixed spice

1 oz (30 g) butter
1 oz (30 g) demerara
   sugar
1 oz (30 g) plain flour

Mix together apple, sultanas and spice and put into a well-greased pie dish. Cream together butter and demerara sugar and work in flour until mixture is crumbly. Spread over apple mixture and bake in a hot oven for 10 minutes, then in a moderate oven until apple is soft and the top is brown (about 15 minutes).

208. Bread and Butter Pudding   Serves 4–6

8–10 slices of bread
   and butter
3 oz (90 g) dried fruit
1 oz (30 g) brown sugar

1 pt (6 dl) milk
1 egg, beaten
$\frac{1}{2}$ tsp mixed spice

Cut bread and butter into small pieces. Put a layer, butter side up, in a well-greased pie dish and sprinkle a layer of mixed dried fruit, sugar and spice over. Repeat layers, finishing with bread—butter side up. Beat egg with milk and pour over bread mixture. Leave to stand for 30 minutes, then bake in a moderate oven for 45 minutes.

209. Bread and Marmalade Pudding   Serves 4–6

8 oz (240 g) bread,
   sliced and liberally
   spread with butter
   and marmalade

8 oz (240 g) cooking
   apples, sliced
1 egg, beaten
$\frac{1}{2}$ pt (3 dl) milk
a little brown sugar

Put a layer of bread and marmalade, plain side down, into a well-greased pie dish, then a layer of apples. Repeat layers, finishing with bread and marmalade (plain side up). Beat egg in milk and pour over. Leave to stand for 30 minutes. Sprinkle with sugar and bake in a moderate oven for 45 minutes.

210. Bread and Plum Pudding   Serves 4–6

8–10 slices of bread,
   cut small
1 lb (480 g) plums,
   halved and stoned

2 oz (60 g) sugar
1 oz (30 g) butter

Line bottom and sides of a well-greased pie dish with bread. Place a layer of plums in and sprinkle with sugar. Cover with layer of bread. Repeat layers, finishing with bread. Dot with butter, cover with foil and bake in a moderately hot oven for 1 hour.

211. Bread and Rhubarb Pudding   Serves 4 – 6

4 oz (120 g)   2 oz (60 g) demerara
 breadcrumbs   sugar
1 lb (480 g) rhubarb,   1 oz (30 g) suet
 stewed   1 tsp mixed spice

Mix breadcrumbs, sugar, suet and spice together. Put
a layer of rhubarb into a well-greased pie dish, then a
layer of breadcrumb mixture. Repeat layers, finishing
with breadcrumb mixture. Cover with foil and bake in
a hot oven for 20 minutes. Remove foil and bake for a
further 15 minutes.

212. Chocolate Bread Pudding   Serves 4 – 6

1 tbsp cocoa   1 egg, beaten
3 oz (90 g) breadcrumbs   1 pt (6 dl) milk
2 oz (60 g) sugar $\frac{1}{2}$ tsp vanilla essence

Mix together cocoa, breadcrumbs and sugar. Beat egg
with milk and vanilla essence and pour over breadcrumb mixture. Beat well together then pour into a
well-greased pie dish and bake in a moderate oven for
45 minutes. Serve with hot Chocolate Sauce (as variation of recipe no. 311).

213. Date and Rice Pudding   Serves 4 – 6

4 oz (120 g) dates,   1 egg, beaten
 chopped $\frac{3}{4}$ pt (4 $\frac{1}{2}$ dl) milk
2 oz (60 g) rice   grated nutmeg
2 oz (60 g) sugar

Sprinkle rice into boiling water and simmer for 20
minutes. Strain and mix with all other ingredients.
Turn into a well-greased pie dish and bake in a
moderate oven for about 35 minutes.

214. Banana Custard Bake

Serves 4 – 6

3 bananas
4 oz (120 g) bread,
   broken small
$\frac{1}{2}$ pt (3 dl) milk, hot

For the custard
1 $\frac{1}{2}$ oz (45 g) cornflour
1 oz (30 g) sugar
$\frac{1}{2}$ pt (3 dl) milk
few drops vanilla
   essence
grated lemon rind

Put bread into a saucepan of hot milk and leave to soak for 10 minutes. Make a paste of cornflour, sugar and a little cold milk. Heat remaining milk; remove from heat and gradually stir into paste. Return to saucepan and heat slowly, stirring continuously, until thick. Add vanilla essence and grated lemon rind. Stir custard into the bread and milk and beat. Slice bananas and place in a well-greased pie dish. Pour custard mixture over and bake in a hot oven until brown (15 to 20 minutes).

215. Rhubarb Gingerbread Pudding

Serves 4 – 6

1 lb (480 g) rhubarb, cut
   into short pieces
2 oz (60 g) margarine
2 tbsps treacle
1 tsp ground ginger
1 tsp cinnamon

$\frac{1}{4}$ pt (1 $\frac{1}{2}$ dl) milk
8 oz (240 g) self-raising
   flour
1 egg, beaten
1 tbsp demerara sugar

Put margarine, treacle and spices into saucepan and melt over low heat. Stir in milk and gradually add flour. Add egg and beat well. Pour half into a well-greased 10 × 8 × 2-in (25 × 20 × 5-cm) baking tin. Put rhubarb on top and sprinkle with sugar. Pour remaining mixture over and bake in a moderate oven for 1 hour.

216. Queen of Raspberry Puddings   Serves 4 – 6

1 lb (480 g) raspberries   2 eggs, separated
3 oz (90 g) breadcrumbs   1 pt (6 dl) milk
4 oz (120 g) sugar

Mix breadcrumbs with 1 oz (30 g) sugar. Beat yolks of
eggs, add milk, then pour over breadcrumbs. Leave to
stand for 10 minutes. Put raspberries in a greased pie
dish, sprinkle 1 oz (30 g) sugar over and cover with
breadcrumb mixture. Bake for 20 minutes in a
moderate oven. Beat whites of eggs until stiff, then
gently stir in remaining sugar. Pile egg-white mixture
roughly on the pudding then bake in a very slow oven
until biscuit coloured (about 15 minutes).

217. Jam Sponge Pudding   Serves 4 – 6

8 oz (240 g) jam (or   1 egg, beaten
    stewed fruit, or small   5 oz (150 g) self-raising
    can of fruit)   flour
2 oz (60 g) butter   2 tbsps milk
2 oz (60 g) sugar

Spread jam (or fruit) in bottom of a well-greased pie
dish. Cream together butter and sugar, then beat in
egg, flour and milk. Spread mixture on top of jam (or
fruit) and bake in a moderate oven until golden-brown
(30 to 40 minutes).

218. Lemon Soufflé   Serves 4 – 6

1 lemon   3 oz (90 g) breadcrumbs
1 oz (30 g) butter $\frac{1}{2}$ pt (3 dl) hot milk
2 oz (60 g) sugar   2 eggs, separated

Mix butter, sugar and breadcrumbs, then slowly add
the hot milk, stirring continuously. Leave to stand for
about 10 minutes, then stir in juice and grated rind of
lemon and the yolks of eggs. Beat whites of eggs until
stiff, then fold into mixture. Pour into a well-greased
pie dish and bake in a moderate oven for 20 minutes.

219. Pineapple Soufflé

Serves 4–6

1 small can of
   pineapple, chopped
   small

1 tbsp cornflour
1 tbsp sugar
1 egg, separated

Mix together cornflour and sugar, then blend in yolk of egg and pineapple juice—made up to approximately $\frac{1}{2}$pt (3 dl) with water. Cook in saucepan until thick. Beat white of egg until stiff, then fold into mixture. Stir in the pineapple, then pour into a well-greased pie dish and bake in a moderate oven for 20 minutes.

220. Semolina Soufflé

Serves 4–6

2 oz (60 g) semolina
1 pt (6 dl) milk
2 oz (60 g) sugar
a little grated rind of
   lemon or orange

grated nutmeg
$\frac{1}{2}$ oz (15 g) butter
2 eggs, separated

Pour milk into saucepan, add sugar and gently sprinkle in semolina, stirring well over a low heat until thick. Then stir in grated rind, a little nutmeg, butter and yolks of eggs. Cook for 2 or 3 minutes, then fold in stiffly beaten whites of eggs. Pour into a well-greased pie dish and bake in a moderate oven for 20 minutes.

221. Coffee Soufflé

Serves 4–6

$\frac{1}{2}$pt (3 dl) strong black
   coffee
1 $\frac{1}{2}$oz (45 g) butter
2 oz (60 g) plain flour

1 oz (30 g) sugar
2 eggs, separated

Melt butter and stir in flour. Remove from heat and slowly add coffee, stirring continuously to avoid lumps. Return to heat and cook gently, stirring continuously, for a few minutes until the mixture thickens. Remove from heat, add sugar and yolks of eggs. Mix thoroughly, then fold in stiffly beaten whites of eggs. Pour into a well-greased pie dish and bake in a moderate oven for 20 minutes.

222. Apple Delight (Afal Nice)   Serves 4–6

2 large crisp cooking
  apples, grated
3 tbsps sweetened
  condensed milk

1 oz (30 g) raisins,
  chopped
1 oz (30 g) nuts, chopped

Mix all ingredients together.

223. Apple Sponge   Serves 4–6

1 lb (480 g) cooking
  apples, sliced
4 or 5 slices of stale
  sponge cake, broken
  small

1 oz (30 g) sugar
$\frac{1}{2}$ pt (3 dl) thick custard
1 egg, separated

Simmer apples with sugar and a little water until soft.
Mash, then leave to cool. Put sponge cake into a pie
dish and cover with half of the apples. Make custard,
using the yolk of egg, and pour over apples in pie dish.
Beat white of egg until stiff, then mix with remaining
apples. Beat to a cream and spoon on to custard.

224. Fruit Mould   Serves 4–6

This is best made when there is a glut of fruit.

1 lb (480 g) ripe soft
  fruit
1 pt (6 dl) water

2 oz (60 g) sugar
4 tbsps cornflour

Stew fruit with water and sugar until soft, then mash.
Mix cornflour with fruit, bring to the boil and simmer
for 10 minutes, stirring continuously. Turn into wet
mould and leave to set.

225. Stewed Fruit Pudding   Serves 4 – 6

1 pt (6 dl) hot stewed   several thick slices of
   fruit   bread

Line a greased 2-pt (12-dl) pudding basin with bread.
Pour in the fruit and cover with a bread lid. Place a
saucer on top of the pudding and place a weight in the
saucer. Leave overnight to set.

226. Fruit and Oatmeal Pudding   Serves 4 – 6

8 oz (240 g) stewed   1 oz (30 g) sugar
   damsons or black-   1 dsp cocoa
   currants   a few drops of vanilla
4 oz (120 g) oatmeal,   essence
   soaked overnight in
   $\frac{3}{4}$ pt (4 $\frac{1}{2}$ dl) milk

Stir sugar and cocoa into the oatmeal and milk mixture, then simmer gently, stirring continuously, until
oatmeal is cooked. Remove from heat and stir in vanilla
essence. Put alternate layers of stewed fruit and oatmeal mixture into a wet fruit dish and leave overnight
to set.

6. Cakes

During the Second World War my mother—deter-mined that no enemy action was going to deplete her larder—made cakes from 'national' flour, dried egg, liquid paraffin (instead of fat) saccharin and a few currants. I can remember those cakes well, but find it difficult to describe them. They were remarkable; not exactly sweet, nor exactly tasty, nor exactly anything . . . but they were certainly *large*. We all chewed our way loyally through slice after slice, and one cake served our family of six for a week. I accepted that this was how fruit cakes should be until the day that I was given a slice of cake made by my best friend's mother and I came to know how greedily delicious home-made cakes could be. It didn't take me long to work out that her father being on the Council and her mother working in the Food Office probably had something to do with the fact that they never seemed short of butter and sugar, but it wasn't until I started making cakes myself that I came to understand that delicious cakemaking is not entirely a matter of rich ingredients. My first rock cakes (made at the school cookery class) lived up to their name. We tried eating them on the way home, but ended up throwing them at the dustbins along the way. (They made a very satisfying 'boyng' as they hit the sides.) And my very first fruit cake made at home surpassed anything that my mother had produced because not only was it *large*, but it came from the oven steaming darkly with malevolence and burnt sultanas. Its iron-hard crust defied our sharpest knife, so it was christened 'Bet's Borstal Bake' and fed to the dog.

I have learned a bit since those days, and as I accept that my cake-making talents are extremely limited I tackle no set of cooking directions that calls for any degree of finesse. That concept is well reflected in the following recipes. Not only will they produce cakes that are tasty, cheap and nourishing, you will find that you *can't go wrong with them*. There are very few 'dainties' because we generally prefer cakes that can be cut and carried easily in a lunch box.

227. Mrs Lloyd's Gingerbread

1 tsp ground ginger
3 oz (90 g) margarine
4 oz (120 g) black
   treacle
4 oz (120 g) golden
   syrup
1 tsp ground cloves

1 tsp cinnamon
$\frac{1}{4}$ pt (1 $\frac{1}{2}$ dl) milk
1 egg, beaten
2 oz (60 g) dates,
   chopped
6 oz (180 g) self-raising
   flour

Gently heat margarine, treacle, syrup and spices in a saucepan until runny. Stir in milk, then mix together all ingredients and beat well. Pour into a well-greased baking tin (approx. 11 × 9 × 2 in (27$\frac{1}{2}$ × 22$\frac{1}{2}$ × 5 cm)) and bake in a slow oven for 45 to 60 minutes (until it is just firm to touch). Leave to cool in tin.

228. Fig and Oatmeal Gingerbread

4 oz (120 g) figs,
   chopped
3 oz (90 g) oatmeal
1 tsp ground ginger
2 oz (60 g) margarine
4 oz (120 g) treacle

1 oz (30 g) brown sugar
1 tsp mixed spice
$\frac{1}{4}$ pt (1 $\frac{1}{2}$ dl) milk
1 egg, beaten
5 oz (150 g) self-raising
   flour

Gently heat margarine, treacle, sugar and spices in a saucepan until runny. Stir in milk, then mix together all ingredients and beat well. Pour into a well-greased baking tin (approx. 11 × 9 × 2 in (27$\frac{1}{2}$ × 22$\frac{1}{2}$ × 5 cm)) and cook in a slow oven for about 1 hour (until it is just firm to touch). Leave to cool in tin.

229. Apple Gingerbread

8 oz (240 g) stewed
   apple
1 tsp ground ginger
5 oz (150 g) margarine
4 oz (120 g) golden
   syrup

3 oz (90 g) demerara
   sugar
$\frac{1}{2}$ tsp ground cloves
$\frac{1}{2}$ tsp cinnamon
1 egg, beaten
6 oz (180 g) self-raising
   flour

Gently heat margarine, syrup, sugar and spices until
runny. Stir in the apple, then mix together all ingredients and beat well. Turn into a well-greased baking
tin (approx. 11 × 9 × 2 in (27$\frac{1}{2}$ × 22$\frac{1}{2}$ × 5 cm)) and
cook in a moderate oven for about 45 minutes. Leave to
cool in tin.

230. Somerset Cider Cake

$\frac{1}{4}$ pt (1 $\frac{1}{2}$ dl) cider
4 oz (120 g) margarine
4 oz (120 g) sugar
2 eggs, beaten

8 oz (240 g) plain flour
1 tsp bicarbonate of
   soda
1 tsp grated nutmeg

Cream together margarine and sugar, then beat in
eggs and 4 oz (120 g) flour. Mix bicarbonate of soda,
and grated nutmeg thoroughly with the remaining
flour. Pour cider into margarine, sugar and egg mixture and beat well. Then add remaining flour and beat
well. Turn into a well-greased baking tin (approx. 11 ×
9 × 2 in (27$\frac{1}{2}$ × 22$\frac{1}{2}$ × 5 cm)) and cook in a moderate
oven for about 45 minutes. Cool on a wire tray.

231. Hafod Parkin

2 oz (60 g) margarine
8 oz (240 g) black
    treacle
$\frac{1}{2}$ tsp ground ginger
$\frac{1}{4}$ pt (1$\frac{1}{2}$ dl) milk

$\frac{1}{2}$ tsp bicarbonate of
    soda
$\frac{1}{4}$ tsp salt
6 oz (180 g) oatmeal
3 oz (90 g) wholemeal
    flour

Gently heat margarine, treacle and ground ginger until runny. Stir in milk. Mix bicarbonate of soda and salt thoroughly with oatmeal and flour, then mix together all ingredients and turn into a well-greased baking tin (approx. 11 × 9 × 2 in (27$\frac{1}{2}$ × 22$\frac{1}{2}$ × 5 cm)). Cook in a slow oven until firm (1$\frac{1}{2}$ to 2 hours). Leave in tin to cool.

232. Bran Parkin

2 oz (60 g) bran
3 oz (90 g) margarine
1 oz (30 g) brown sugar
4 oz (120 g) black
    treacle
$\frac{1}{2}$ tsp ground ginger
$\frac{1}{2}$ tsp mixed spice

1 egg, beaten
4 oz (120 g) oatmeal
4 oz (120 g) raisins or
    chopped dates
1 oz (30 g) wholemeal
    flour

Gently heat margarine, sugar, treacle and spices until runny, then beat into the egg and gradually add all other ingredients. Turn into a well-greased baking tin (approx. 11 × 9 × 2 in (27$\frac{1}{2}$ × 22$\frac{1}{2}$ × 5 cm)) and cook in a slow oven until firm to the touch (1$\frac{1}{2}$ to 2 hours). Leave in tin to cool.

233. Keep-if-you-can Fruit Cake (without eggs)

12 oz (360 g) mixed
   dried fruit, including
   glace cherries and
   candied peel
3 oz (90 g) margarine
8 oz (240 g) plain flour

4 oz (120 g) sugar
1 tsp bicarbonate of
   soda
a pinch of salt
$\frac{1}{4}$ pt (1 $\frac{1}{2}$ dl) milk
2 dsps vinegar

Rub margarine into flour then mix in sugar and dried fruit. Dissolve bicarbonate of soda and salt in milk. Quickly stir in vinegar, then beat into flour and fruit mixture. Turn into a well-greased 7-in (17$\frac{1}{2}$-cm) cake tin and bake in a moderate oven for 15 minutes, then in a slow oven for 1 hour. Leave to cool in tin.

234. Plate Fruit Cake (Teison Blat)

Baking this cake on an earthenware plate seems to increase its fruity flavour. The cake is crisp at the edges and moist in the centre. It also means that you can bake a cake when the only space available in the oven is a narrow gap between shelves.

4 oz (120 g) margarine
4 oz (120 g) sugar
2 eggs, beaten
6 oz (180 g) self-raising
   flour

4 oz (120 g) mixed dried
   fruit
$\frac{1}{2}$ tsp mixed spice
$\frac{1}{2}$ tsp grated nutmeg
$\frac{1}{4}$ pt (1 $\frac{1}{2}$ dl) (approx.)
   milk

Cream together margarine and sugar. Add eggs, then all other dry ingredients and mix well together. Gradually add enough milk to make a fairly soft mixture. Spread over a well-greased 10-in (25-cm) plate and cook in a moderate oven for 10 minutes, then in a slow oven for 40 to 45 minutes. Leave to cool on plate.

235. Sour Milk Raisin Cake

$\frac{1}{4}$ pt (1 $\frac{1}{2}$ dl) sour milk
4 oz (120 g) raisins
2 oz (60 g) margarine
8 oz (240 g) wholemeal
   flour

2 oz (60 g) brown sugar
$\frac{1}{2}$ tsp bicarbonate of
   soda

Rub margarine into flour, stir in sugar and raisins. Dissolve bicarbonate of soda in milk and beat into mixture. Turn into a well-greased 7-in (17$\frac{1}{2}$-cm) cake tin and bake in a hot oven for 5 minutes, then in a slow oven for 1 hour. Cool on a wire tray.

236. Dad's Bread Pudding

This is a very good way of using up stale bread.

12 oz (360 g) bread,
   broken and soaked in
   water for a few
   hours or overnight
6 oz (180 g) mixed dried
   fruit

4 oz (120 g) lard (or suet)
2 oz (60 g) brown sugar
2 tsps mixed spice
1 tbsp treacle (or golden
   syrup)
1 egg, beaten

Drain bread, squeeze dry and mix with lard (or suet) and all dry ingredients. Stir in treacle and egg and mix well. Turn into a well-greased shallow baking tin (approx. 11 × 9 × 2 in (27$\frac{1}{2}$ × 22$\frac{1}{2}$ × 5 cm)) and bake in a moderate oven for 1 hour. Leave to cool in tin.

237. Welsh Griddle Cakes

4 oz (120 g) margarine
8 oz (240 g) self-raising
    flour
4 oz (120 g) currants
3 oz (90 g) sugar

$\frac{1}{2}$ tsp mixed spice
a pinch of salt
1 egg, beaten
a little milk

Rub margarine into flour, then add all other ingredients—using enough milk to make soft dough. Knead lightly, then turn onto floured board and roll out to about $\frac{1}{4}$ in (6 mm) thick. Cut into rounds and bake on a moderately hot greased griddle (or in an iron frying pan) until slightly brown (about 5 minutes each side). Cool on a wire tray.

238. Caraway Griddle Cakes

2 tsps caraway seeds
4 oz (120 g) margarine
8 oz (240 g) self-raising
    flour

2 oz (60 g) sugar
a little milk

Rub margarine into flour, then add all other ingredients, using enough milk to make soft (but not sticky) dough. Turn on to a floured board and knead lightly. Roll out to about $\frac{1}{4}$ in (6 mm) thick and cut into rounds. Bake on a moderately hot greased griddle (or in an iron frying pan) until slightly brown (about 5 minutes each side). Cool on a wire tray.

239. Doughnuts Without Yeast

This is my mother-in-law's recipe. When asked what was the imperial or metric capacity of her teacup I was informed tartly that it didn't matter what size the teacup was, so long as you used the same cup for the flour and milk.

2 teacups self-raising flour	1 teacup milk
2 tbsps sugar	3 tsps baking powder
2 eggs	sugar for coating
	jam for filling

Mix together all ingredients (except sugar for coating and jam), adding the baking powder last. Beat well. Drop dessertspoons of mixture into hot deep fat. Cook for a few minutes until brown all over. Drain and put on to paper spread with sugar. Leave to cool, then roll in sugar, pull slightly open and put in jam.

240. Almond Cakes (Teison Sioned)

a little almond flavouring	
2 – 3 tbsps red jam	For the pastry
2 oz (60 g) butter	3 oz (90 g) margarine
2 oz (60 g) sugar	6 oz (180 g) plain flour
1 egg, beaten	a little milk
2 oz (60 g) self-raising flour	

Rub margarine into flour and add milk to make stiff dough. Roll out and cut into rounds and line patty tins. Into each pastry round put 1 teaspoon of jam. Cream together butter and sugar; add the egg and flavouring, then beat in the flour. Cover each pastry round with 1 teaspoonful of mixture and bake in a hot oven for 10 to 15 minutes. Cool on a wire tray.

241. Sponge Cake with One Egg

1 egg, beaten
5 oz (150 g) plain flour
3 oz (90 g) sugar
1 tsp cream of tartar

1 tsp bicarbonate of
  soda
$\frac{1}{4}$ pt (1 $\frac{1}{2}$ dl) milk
1 oz (30 g) butter,
  melted

Mix together flour, sugar and cream of tartar. Dissolve
bicarbonate of soda in milk and beat into the egg. Pour
into the flour mixture and beat well—adding the
melted butter. Turn into two greased 7-in (17$\frac{1}{2}$-cm)
sandwich tins or one greased 7-in (17$\frac{1}{2}$-cm) cake tin.
Bake in a moderate oven for about 15 minutes (if in two
tins) or about 25 minutes if in one tin. Cool on a wire
tray.

242. Cheap Chocolate Cake

1 tbsp cocoa
2 oz (60 g) margarine
2 oz (60 g) sugar
1 oz (30 g) treacle
3 tbsps milk

1 tsp bicarbonate of
  soda
1 egg, beaten
6 oz (180 g) plain flour

Gently heat all ingredients except bicarbonate of soda,
egg and flour, until runny. Mix with the egg and
gradually beat in flour and bicarbonate of soda. Turn
into a well-greased 7-in (17$\frac{1}{2}$-cm) cake tin and cook in a
moderate oven for 10 minutes then in a slow oven for
30 minutes. Cool on a wire tray.

(This cake can be enlivened by slicing in two and
sandwiching with butter cream—as in recipe no. 243,
but flavoured with 1 teaspoon cocoa and a few drops of
vanilla essence.)

243. Orange Butter-cream Cake

1 orange
4 oz (120 g) margarine
4 oz (120 g) sugar
2 eggs, beaten
5 oz (150 g) self-raising
    flour

For the butter cream
2 oz (60 g) butter
3 oz (90 g) icing sugar
1 dsp orange juice

Cream together margarine and sugar; add eggs and
beat in the flour, grated rind of the orange and 1 tablespoon of juice. Turn into a well-greased 7-in (17½-cm)
cake tin and bake in a moderate oven until golden
brown (about 30 minutes). Cool on a wire tray. Blend
together the butter and icing sugar, and add the
orange juice. Mix well until smooth and creamy. Slice
cake in two and sandwich with butter-icing.

(Any orange juice left may be mixed with icing sugar
and used to cover top of cake.)

244. Jam and Coconut Sandwich Cake

4 tbsps jam
3 oz (90 g) desiccated
    coconut
4 oz (120 g) margarine

4 oz (120 g) sugar
2 eggs, beaten
5 oz (150 g) self-raising
    flour

Cream together margarine and sugar, add the eggs and
beat well. Mix together the flour and 2 oz (60 g) coconut
and gradually beat into the egg mixture. Spread in a
well-greased Swiss roll tin and bake in a moderate
oven until golden-brown (about 25 minutes). Cool on a
wire tray. Slice the cake in two and sandwich with 2
tablespoons of jam. Spread remaining jam on top, then
sprinkle remaining coconut over.

7. Scones and Bread

Making bread is part of my normal domestic routine —like doing the washing. I would no more think of buying bread from a shop than I would of sending my clothes to the laundry. I bake two 1-lb loaves approximately three times in two weeks and—with my corner-cutting method—the whole operation from getting out your mixing bowl to finally lifting the loaves from the oven, needn't take more than $2\frac{1}{2}$ hours.

The breads made without yeast are quicker to prepare and cook, but they don't keep so well. I have quoted dried yeast for my basic bread recipe because I have no experience of using fresh yeast, but my mother used to follow a similar recipe, using fresh yeast, and had very good results; moreover her bread always looked better than mine—lighter and crustier.(I prefer to use dried yeast because it is easier to obtain than fresh, and a large tin of it can be stored conveniently.) I have made bread using natural or 'wild' yeasts and

159

they work quite well, but the finished loaf is smaller and denser, with a distinctive 'tang' to it, and this is not a method you can suddenly decide to use, because the yeast needs at least three days to grow. (To explain briefly: you make a 'starter' by putting two table-spoons each of wholemeal flour and warm water into a jar, cover it with a cloth and leave for twenty-four hours. Then over the following two or three days you 'feed' it with a little more wholemeal flour and warm water until it is a spongy, slowly bubbling mass, and ready to use. This old method of making yeast is coming back into fashion and is sometimes called 'sourdough' cookery.)

But whatever method of breadmaking you prefer, the chances are that you will turn out a tastier, 'nuttier', more wholesome and nutritious loaf than any you can buy in a shop. It will also be cheaper. In the following recipes I refer, where appropriate, to 'wholemeal flour' because I think most of you will gather what I mean. But the term is, strictly speaking, a contradiction. (I.e. 'wholemeal' is the entire ground product of the grain, which contains the bran, germ and flour. 'Flour' contains no bran and little germ.) Undoubtedly the best meal for your breadmaking is that from freshly-ground whole wheat, but it is not readily available and most of us have to make do with the bags of stuff which bear labels like 'Wheatmeal flour' or 'Brown Bread Flour'. I generally look for something labelled '100% wholemeal'—and hope for the best.

Making bread is not so difficult, and the normal working temperature of your kitchen is warm enough for the rising dough. In fact, in our experience, the only thing that seems to affect the success of breadmaking is the mood of the maker. If I am in a bad temper the loaves don't rise so well. So, with my dough recipes, you can be as slap-happy as you like with quantities, method or temperatures ... but for goodness sake, don't glare at it!

160

245. Plain Scones

White scones
about ¼ pt (1 ½ dl) sour
    milk
8 oz (240 g) plain flour
1 tsp bicarbonate of
    soda
a pinch of salt
1 ½ oz (45 g) margarine
1 ½ oz (45 g) sugar

Brown scones
about ¼ pt (1 ½ dl) sour
    milk
8 oz (240 g) wholemeal
    flour
1 ½ tsps bicarbonate of
    soda
a pinch of salt
2 oz (60 g) margarine
2 oz (60 g) brown sugar

Mix together all dry ingredients. Rub in margarine and add sour milk to make soft dough. Roll on floured board to about ¾ in (18 mm) thick and cut into rounds, squares or triangles. Brush with milk and place on a lightly greased and floured baking sheet. Cook in a hot oven until firm to the touch and lightly browned (about 15 to 20 minutes). Cool on a wire tray.

VARIATIONS

Sweet

Date and Treacle: Use half quantity milk and half quantity margarine. Add 2 oz (60 g) dates, chopped. Replace sugar with 1 tbsp warmed black treacle and 1 tsp mixed spice.
Marmalade: Replace sugar with 1 tbsp marmalade.
Fruit: Add 2 oz (60 g) dried fruit.
Coconut: Add 2 oz (60 g) desiccated coconut.

Savoury

Onion and Curry: Replace sugar with 2 oz (60 g) chopped fried onions or shallots, and 1 tsp curry powder.
Herb: Replace sugar with 1 tsp dried mixed herbs and a pinch of cayenne pepper. These are best eaten whilst still warm, with butter and cheese, or as an extra filler with a meat dish.

Cheese: Replace sugar and salt with 2 oz (60 g) grated cheese and $\frac{1}{2}$ tsp yeast extract.
Bacon: Replace sugar and salt with 2 oz (60 g) chopped fried bacon.

246. Dripping Scones (Carmel Scones)

6 oz (180 g) wholemeal
  flour
2 oz (60 g) plain flour
1 tsp bicarbonate of
  soda

a pinch of salt
3 oz (90 g) dripping
1 tsp vinegar
1 egg, beaten

Mix together all dry ingredients then rub in dripping. Mix vinegar with egg and stir into flour mixture to make a firm dough. Roll out on floured board to a round shape about $\frac{1}{2}$ in (12 mm) thick; cut into 6 or 8 segments, place on a lightly greased and floured baking sheet and cook in a hot oven until firm to the touch and lightly browned (15 to 20 minutes). Cool on a wire tray.

247. Cheese and Egg Scones

2 oz (60 g) cheese,
  grated
6 oz (180 g) wholemeal
  flour
3 tsps baking powder

a little salt
4 tbsps milk
1 egg, beaten
a little extra milk

Mix the cheese with all dry ingredients. Beat egg with milk and pour into wholemeal mixture to make soft dough. Roll out on floured board to about $\frac{1}{2}$ in (12 mm) thick, cut into rounds and place on a lightly greased and floured baking sheet. Brush with milk and cook in a hot oven until firm to the touch and lightly browned (10 to 15 minutes). Cool on a wire tray.

248. Cheese and Potato Scones

2 oz (60 g) cheese,
  grated
6 oz (180 g) boiled
  potatoes, mashed
¼ pt (1 ½ dl) milk
  (approx.)

1 ½ oz (45 g) margarine,
  melted
½ tsp yeast extract
3 oz (90 g) self-raising
  flour
a little extra milk

Mix together all ingredients to make stiff dough. Roll
out on floured board to about ½ in (12 mm) thick. Cut
into rounds or squares, brush with milk and place on a
lightly greased and floured baking sheet. Cook in a hot
oven until golden brown (10 to 15 minutes). Cool on a
wire tray.

249. Herb and Potato Scones

1 tsp mixed dried herbs
4 oz (120 g) boiled
  potatoes, mashed
4 oz (120 g) plain flour
2 tsps baking powder

cayenne pepper, salt
2 oz (60 g) butter
4 tbsps milk (approx.)
a little extra milk

Mix together all dry ingredients, rub in butter and add
milk to make soft dough. Roll out on a floured board to
about ½ in (12 mm) thick. Cut into rounds and place on a
lightly greased and floured baking sheet. Brush over
with milk and cook in a hot oven until browned (15 to 20
minutes). Cool on a wire tray.

250. Quick White Rolls (without yeast)

8 oz (240 g) plain flour
3 tsps baking powder
a pinch of salt

¼ pt (1 ½ dl) sour milk
  (approx.)
a little extra milk

Mix together all dry ingredients and stir in sour milk to
make soft dough. Break into small pieces and form into
rolls. Brush with milk and place on a greased and
floured baking sheet. Cook in a hot oven until brown (10
to 15 minutes). Cool on a wire tray.

251. **Quick White Bread** (without yeast)

1 lb (480 g) plain flour	2 oz (60 g) margarine
4 tsps baking powder	1 pt milk
$\frac{1}{2}$ tsp salt	

Mix together all dry ingredients. Melt margarine in saucepan, add the milk and heat until warm. Pour into the flour, mix well then knead briefly with a well-floured hand (best to keep one clean). Turn into a well-greased and floured 1-lb (or 500-g) loaf tin and bake in a moderately hot oven for 35 to 45 minutes. Cool on a wire tray.

252. **Quick Oatmeal Bread** (without yeast)

2 oz (60 g) oatmeal	$\frac{1}{2}$ tsp salt
8 oz (240 g) plain flour	1 oz (30 g) margarine
1 tsp bicarbonate of soda	$\frac{1}{4}$ pt (1 $\frac{1}{2}$ dl) sour milk (approx.)

Mix together all dry ingredients. Rub in margarine and add sour milk to make soft dough. Turn on to floured board and, with a well-floured hand, knead until smooth and pliable. Put into a well-greased and floured 1-lb (or 500-g) loaf tin and bake in a moderately hot oven for about 30 minutes. Cool on a wire tray.

253. **Fruit Bread** (without yeast)(1)

12 oz (360 g) plain flour	1 tsp mixed spice
4 oz (120 g) demerara sugar	1 tsp bicarbonate of soda
4 oz (120 g) mixed dried fruit (including candied peel), chopped	1 tsp cream of tartar
	a pinch of salt
	$\frac{1}{4}$ pt (1 $\frac{1}{2}$ dl) milk

Mix together all dry ingredients, then stir in milk and beat well. Turn into a well-greased and floured 1-lb (or 500-g) loaf tin, and bake in a moderate oven for 45 minutes to 1 hour. Cool on a wire tray.

254. Fruit Bread (without yeast)(2)

4 oz (120 g) mixed dried
  fruit
12 oz (360 g) self-raising
  flour
2 oz (60 g) demerara
  sugar

2 oz (60 g) nuts, chopped
1 tsp mixed spice
a pinch of salt
$\frac{1}{4}$ pt (1 $\frac{1}{2}$ dl) milk
1 egg, beaten
1 tbsp golden syrup

Mix together all dry ingredients. Beat milk into egg and
pour into mixture. Add golden syrup and mix well.
Turn into well-greased and floured 1-lb (or 500-g) loaf
tin. Bake in a moderate oven for about 1 hour. Cool on a
wire tray.

255. Cold Tea Bread (Dan Hayman's Brack) (without yeast)

8 oz (240 g) candied
  peel, chopped, mixed
  with 4 oz (120 g)
  sugar, and soaked
  overnight in $\frac{1}{4}$ pt
  (1 $\frac{1}{2}$ dl) cold tea

8 oz (240 g) self-raising
  flour
1 egg, beaten

Mix together all ingredients and turn into a well-
greased 8-in (20-cm) square baking tin. Cook in a
moderate oven for 1 hour. Cool on a wire tray.

256. Basic Bread (Bara Hafod)

$1\frac{1}{2}$ lb (720 g) wholemeal
  flour
8 oz (240 g) plain flour

1 tsp salt
3 tsps sugar
4 tsps dried yeast

Mix together flours and salt. Put sugar and about $\frac{1}{4}$ pt ($1\frac{1}{2}$ dl) tepid water into a jug, sprinkle yeast in and stir. Cover with a cloth and leave until frothy (about 15 to 20 minutes). Add tepid water to make up to 1 pt (6 dl) and pour into flour mixture. Using one hand, mix until dough is in one pliable lump (with none sticking to the bowl). If necessary adjust texture by adding flour or tepid water. Knead for a few minutes, divide in two, knead into shape and place in two well-greased and floured 1-lb (or 500-g) loaf tins. Cover with a cloth and leave to rise until dough is just over the top of the tins (usually 1 to $1\frac{1}{2}$ hours). Bake in a hot oven for 5 minutes, then in a moderate oven until tins sound hollow when tapped on the bottom (about 40 minutes). Remove from tins and return (upside down) to oven for about 5 minutes to crisp. Cool on a wire tray.

VARIATIONS

a . *Wholemeal Bread:* Use 2 lb (960 g) wholemeal flour instead of $1\frac{1}{2}$ lb (720 g) wholemeal and 8 oz (240 g) plain.
b . *White Bread:* Use 2 lb (960 g) plain flour instead of $1\frac{1}{2}$ lb (720 g) wholemeal and 8 oz (240 g) plain.

257. Fruit Malt Loaf

This is made with one quarter of the Basic Bread dough and can be baked in the same tin and at the same time—separated from the plain dough with foil or greased paper. The malt loaf will need longer cooking upside down than the plain dough.

2 oz (60 g) sultanas
1 oz (30 g) candied peel, chopped
2 dsps malt extract

8 oz (240 g) Bara Hafod dough (see preceding recipe)

Pull bread dough into a pancake in the bottom of the mixing bowl. Spoon on malt extract and add candied peel and sultanas. Using one hand, mix thoroughly together, then turn into a well-greased and floured bread tin (either an 8-oz (or 250-g) tin or half of a 1-lb (or 500-g) tin). Cover with a cloth and leave to rise for $1\frac{1}{2}$ hours. (It may not reach the top of the tin.) Bake in a hot oven for 5 minutes, then in a moderate oven for 45 minutes. Remove from tin and return (upside down) to oven for 10 to 15 minutes. Cool on a wire tray.

258. Lardy Cake

4 oz (120 g) lard
8 oz (240 g) white bread dough (see variation b. of Basic Bread recipe no. 256)

3 oz (90 g) sugar
2 oz (60 g) currants
1 tsp mixed spice
a little milk

Roll dough into an oblong. Dot with lard, sprinkle with sugar, currants and a little spice. Fold in three and roll out again. Repeat this process until all dry ingredients are used (except a little sugar), then fold in three to form a flat roll. Brush with milk, sprinkle with sugar and leave to rise for about 30 minutes. Place on a greased and floured baking sheet and bake in a moderate oven for 30 to 40 minutes. Cool on a wire tray.

259. Currant Bread (Bara Brith)

This bread is traditionally cut very thin.

8 oz (240 g) currants
2 oz (60 g) candied peel,
  chopped
1 lb (480 g) plain flour

1 tsp mixed spice
a pinch of salt
2 tsps sugar
2 tsps dried yeast

Mix together all ingredients except sugar and yeast. Put sugar and about ¼ pt (1½ dl) tepid water into a jug, sprinkle with yeast and stir. Cover with a cloth and leave until frothy (about 15 to 20 minutes). Add tepid water to make up to ½ pt (3 dl) and pour into flour mixture. Using one hand, mix until dough is in one pliable lump (with none sticking to the bowl). If necessary adjust texture by adding flour or tepid water. Knead for a few minutes, then place in a well-greased and floured 1-lb (or 500-g) loaf tin. Cover with a cloth and leave to rise until dough is above the top of tin (usually 45 minutes to 1 hour). Bake in a hot oven for 5 minutes, then in a moderate oven for 40 minutes. Cool on a wire tray.

260. Apple Bread (Bara Afal)

8 oz (240 g) stewed
  apple, pulped and
  slightly warm
8 oz (240 g) wholemeal
  flour

8 oz (240 g) plain flour
½ tsp salt
¼ tsp ground cloves
3 tsps sugar
3 tsps dried yeast

Mix together flours, salt and cloves. Put sugar and 4 tablespoons tepid water into a jug, sprinkle with yeast and stir. Cover with a cloth and leave until frothy (about 15 to 20 minutes). Stir in apple, then pour into flour mixture. Then follow method for currant bread (previous recipe). Bake in a hot oven for 5 minutes, then in a moderate oven for 45 to 50 minutes. Cool on a wire tray.

8. Biscuits and Bonk Bars

Once you have sampled some home-made biscuits you won't be very eager to go back to the commercial variety. There is just no comparison for taste and cost, and the varieties you can introduce are infinite.

I don't mind admitting that Alan makes better biscuits than I do. He never follows any recipe—just throws flour and sugar into a bowl and uses some sort of instinct to determine varieties and quantities of ingredients. When I persuaded him to write down a typical basic biscuit recipe he grabbed the nearest piece of paper (it happened to be the *Radio Times*) and scribbled it along one margin. I still have that page of the *Radio Times* (I have consulted it when making biscuits ever since) and I have faithfully copied out the

scrawl from the margin to appear in this book as recipe
no. 261.

Those of you who are old club cyclists know all about
bonk bars. But as I cannot assume that you are *all* old
club cyclists I had better give an explanation. A condition of weary, knee-wobbling exhaustion known as 'the
bonk' is sometimes reached by cyclists who have been
(a) all day in the saddle, or (b) 'honking' (standing on the
pedals) uphill after a hard day's work, or (c) cycling
when they are unfit—and this condition can be
instantly relieved by collapsing on to the roadside and
eating a rich source of sugar. Every cyclist has his own
pet variety of 'bonk bar' (a stick of barley sugar or a
fruit and nut chocolate bar being favourites) and Alan
and I never go out on the bikes without some form of
bonk bar in our saddle bags.

When I worked as a typist in Llanrwst, my five-mile
homeward journey saw me climbing from sea level in
the town to 1,000 feet above sea level to our cottage on
the moors. After a particularly exhausting day at the
typewriter 'the bonk' used to overtake me about half-
way up through the Soflen woodlands, where there is a
very old and accommodating milestone. Over the years
I have eaten bonk bars in many diverse situations—but
none do I remember with such affection as my milestone perch in the evening stillness of the woods on the
B5113 from Llanrwst to Cernioge.

261. Alan's Basic Biscuits

2 oz (60 g) butter
3 oz (90 g) wholemeal
    flour
2 oz (60 g) sugar
1 oz (30 g) oatmeal

1 oz (30 g) desiccated
    coconut
$\frac{1}{2}$ oz (15 g) nuts,
    chopped (or currants)
1 tbsp milk

Rub butter into flour then mix with all other ingredients. Roll out thinly on a well-floured board. (Frequent flouring of the rolling pin will be necessary.) Cut into small rounds and bake on a well-greased baking sheet in a slow oven for 45 to 55 minutes. Remove carefully from baking sheet (with a fish slice) and cool on a wire tray.

262. Coconut and Oatmeal Crunchies

4 oz (120 g) desiccated
    coconut
4 oz (120 g) oatmeal
4 oz (120 g) wholemeal
    flour
4 oz (120 g) margarine

4 oz (120 g) brown sugar
2 tbsps golden syrup
1 tsp mixed spice
1 egg, beaten
1 tsp bicarbonate of
    soda

Mix together coconut, oatmeal and flour. Gently heat margarine, sugar, golden syrup and spice in a saucepan until runny. Remove from heat and pour in egg. Dissolve bicarbonate of soda in 1 tablespoon hot water and add to egg mixture, then pour into coconut mixture and stir well. Place tablespoons of mixture on a well-greased baking sheet and cook in a moderate oven for about 15 minutes. Cool on a wire tray.

263. Coconut Porridge Biscuits

$\frac{1}{2}$ breakfast cup
  desiccated coconut
2 breakfast cups rolled
  oats
4 oz (120 g) margarine
$\frac{1}{2}$ breakfast cup sugar

1 tbsp golden syrup
$\frac{1}{2}$ breakfast cup
  wholemeal flour
$\frac{1}{2}$ tsp bicarbonate of
  soda

Gently heat margarine, sugar and syrup in a saucepan until runny. Mix flour and bicarbonate of soda well, then mix together all ingredients and spread in a well-greased Swiss roll tin. Bake in a moderate oven for about 45 minutes. Mark into slices then leave to cool in tin.

264. Hiraethog Oatcakes

6 oz (180 g) oatmeal
1 oz (30 g) wholemeal
  flour

a pinch of salt

Mix together all ingredients and add enough water to make fairly stiff dough. Turn on to a well-floured board and roll out very thin. Cut into rounds and bake on a lightly greased moderately hot griddle (or in an iron frying pan) until very slightly browned on each side. Remove carefully with a fish slice and cool on a wire tray.

265. Oat Slices

4 oz (120 g) rolled oats
4 oz (120 g) wholemeal
  flour
4 oz (120 g) brown sugar
1 tsp baking powder

4 oz (120 g) margarine
1 egg, beaten

Filling suggestions:
  banana, dates, nuts

Mix all dry ingredients together, then rub in margarine. Stir egg in to make stiff dough. Divide in two and roll each piece on a well-floured board to about $\frac{1}{4}$ in (6 mm) thick and of equal size and shape. Put one piece into a well-greased Swiss roll tin and cover it with sliced banana, chopped dates, chopped nuts, or a combination of these. Lay the other piece of dough on top, press lightly together and bake in a moderate oven until a golden brown (about 30 minutes). Mark into slices and leave to cool in tin.

266. Chocolate Oatcakes

1 tbsp cocoa
2 oz (60 g) rolled oats
2 oz (60 g) wholemeal
  flour

2 oz (60 g) sugar
2 oz (60 g) butter

Mix all the dry ingredients together, then rub in butter. Work with the hand until dough is in one lump. Roll out on floured board, then press into a well-greased Swiss roll tin. Bake in a slow oven for about 45 minutes. Mark into slices, and leave to cool in tin.

267. Parkin Biscuits

4 oz (120 g) self-raising
  flour
1 ½ oz (45 g) margarine
2 oz (60 g) oatmeal

1 oz (30 g) brown sugar
1 tsp mixed spice
3 oz (90 g) golden syrup,
  warm

Mix together all ingredients. With floured hands make
into 8 or 10 balls and place on a greased baking sheet,
with at least 2 in (50 mm) between. Flatten to about ½ in
(12 mm) thick and cook in a slow oven for about 1 hour.
Cool on a wire tray.

268. Date and Ginger Flapjacks

2 oz (60 g) dates,
  chopped
1 tsp ground ginger
3 oz (90 g) margarine

2 oz (60 g) Barbados
  sugar
2 oz (60 g) golden syrup
6 oz (180 g) rolled oats

Gently heat margarine, sugar, golden syrup and
ground ginger in a saucepan until runny. Mix with
dates and rolled oats, then spread in a well-greased
Swiss roll tin and bake in a moderate oven for about 25
minutes. Mark into slices, then leave to cool in tin.

269. Capel Garmon Biscuits

Only the yolk of the egg is really required for these biscuits, but if I have no immediate use for the white I include it in the biscuit mix and add the extra 1 oz (30 g) flour.

Similar West Country biscuits, with saffron, are known as Easter Cakes.

1 egg (or yolk only)	2 oz (60 g) currants
5 oz (150 g) margarine	1 tsp mixed spice
7 oz (210 g) (or 8 oz: 240 g) plain flour	a few drops oil of Cassia
4 oz (120 g) sugar	

Rub margarine into flour, then mix in all other ingredients (combining the oil of Cassia with the egg). Roll out on a well-floured board to $\frac{1}{4}$ in (6 mm) thick, or less, and cut into rounds. Bake on a floured baking sheet in a moderately hot oven for 10 to 15 minutes. Cool on a wire tray.

270. Potato and Nut Biscuits

2 oz (60 g) boiled potatoes, mashed	2 oz (60 g) oatmeal
1 oz (30 g) nuts, chopped	2 oz (60 g) sugar
2 oz (60 g) margarine	a few drops of almond essence
2 oz (60 g) wholemeal flour	

Rub margarine into flour, then add oatmeal and sugar. Mix the potato with the almond essence, then with the hand work into flour mixture. Roll out dough on a well-floured board to about $\frac{1}{4}$ in (6 mm) thick and cut into rounds. Sprinkle nuts over and bake on a well-greased baking sheet in a slow oven for about 45 minutes. Leave to cool on sheet.

271. Cheese Snacks

2 oz (60 g) cheese,
grated
4 oz (120 g) wholemeal
flour

cayenne pepper
2 oz (60 g) margarine
1 egg, beaten

Mix together flour and cayenne pepper. Rub in margarine then mix with cheese and egg. Knead to a stiff paste and turn on to a floured board. Roll out to about $\frac{1}{4}$ in (6 mm) thick and cut into rounds. Cook on a greased and floured baking sheet in a moderate oven for 10 to 15 minutes. Leave to cool on sheet.

272. Cheese Fingers

2 oz (60 g) cheese,
grated
2 oz (60 g) plain flour

2 oz (60 g) margarine
cayenne pepper

Mix together all ingredients until dough is smooth. Roll out on a well-floured board and cut into narrow strips. Cook on a greased and floured baking sheet in a hot oven until golden brown (about 10 minutes). Cool on a wire tray.

273. Cheese and Walnut Biscuits (Aunt Daisy's Canasta Night Cookies)

3 oz (90 g) cheese,
grated
2 oz (60 g) walnuts,
chopped
3 oz (90 g) margarine

3 oz (90 g) wholemeal
flour
cayenne pepper
a little milk

Rub the margarine into the flour. Add the cheese, 1 oz (30 g) walnuts and the pepper. Mix together well. Turn on to a floured board and roll to about $\frac{1}{4}$ in (6 mm) thick. Cut into rounds, brush with milk and sprinkle remaining nuts over. Cook on a greased baking sheet in a moderate oven for about 20 minutes. Cool on a wire tray.

274. Savoury Biscuits

1 tsp yeast extract
3 oz (90 g) dripping

6 oz (180 g) wholemeal
flour

Rub the dripping into the flour and add water to make a soft dough. Roll out on a floured board and spread a thin coat of yeast extract over. Fold and roll out again. Repeat until all yeast extract is used, then roll out very thin and cut into rounds or fingers. Bake on a greased baking sheet in a moderate oven until crisp and brown (about 15 minutes). Cool on a wire tray.

275. Date and Nut Bonk Bar

3 oz (90 g) dates,
chopped
3 oz (90 g) nuts, chopped

1 lb (480 g) demerara
sugar
2 oz (60 g) butter
4 tbsps evaporated milk

Gently heat sugar, butter and milk in a saucepan, stirring continuously, until the mixture thickens. Remove from heat and beat hard until it becomes creamy. Stir in dates and nuts, then turn into a well-greased Swiss roll tin. Mark out into handy bar size whilst still warm. Leave to cool in tin.

276. Chocolate Oat Bonk Bar

1 tbsp cocoa
8 oz (240 g) oatcakes (or
digestive or similar
biscuits), broken very
small

2 oz (60 g) margarine
2 oz (60 g) sugar
1 egg, beaten
a few drops vanilla
essence

Gently heat margarine, sugar and cocoa in a saucepan, stirring continuously, until runny. Add the egg and continue cooking over a low heat for 5 minutes. Remove from heat, then stir in vanilla essence and oatcakes. Mix well, then spread mixture in a Swiss roll tin. Mark out into handy bar size whilst still warm. Leave to cool in tin.

277. Coconut Bonk Bar

12 oz [360 g] desiccated
   coconut
1 lb [480 g] sugar

$\frac{1}{4}$ pt [1 $\frac{1}{2}$ dl] milk
$\frac{1}{2}$ tsp cream of tartar

Gently heat sugar, milk and cream of tartar in a sauce-pan, and bring to the boil, stirring continuously, until sugar is dissolved. Simmer for 5 minutes, stirring occasionally, then remove from heat and stir in the coconut. Mix well, then turn into a well-greased Swiss roll tin. Mark out into handy bar size whilst still warm. Leave to cool in tin.

278. Nut and Raisin Treacle Toffee (soft or brittle)

nuts and raisins,
   chopped
8 oz [240 g] black
   treacle

2 oz [60 g] butter
2 oz [60 g] Barbados
   sugar
1 tsp vinegar

Gently heat treacle, butter and sugar in a saucepan and bring to the boil, stirring continuously. Then simmer for about 20 minutes [for soft toffee] or 30 minutes [for brittle toffee], stirring occasionally. Cover the bottom of a well-greased Swiss roll tin with a mixture of nuts and raisins. Remove toffee from heat, add the vinegar, stir well, then pour toffee into the prepared tin. When the toffee is almost cold, cut into pieces and wrap individually in greaseproof paper.

9. Preserves

By the end of summer the shelves of my storecupboard at Hafod would be filled with gleaming jars of fruit and jam—and as soon as the garden produce had been gathered and preserved I turned with acquisitive eyes to the trees upon the moor and the hedgerows along the lane. (I have included a recipe for blackberry jam because although the more popular 'bramble jelly' is certainly delicious, you can fill more jars per pound of fruit if you make jam with it.) Even the most unlikely looking berries and nuts would catch my attention and set me asking myself 'What can I do with that?' (mind you, some of the things I have done with acorns and beechmast are best forgotten), and it wasn't until the last of the wild foods had been taken, either by me or the birds and squirrels, and the naked hedges reared starkly against the November sky that I sat back primly in my kitchen chair and enjoyed that 'all is safely gathered in' feeling.

In January my preserving pan would be in use once again to make marmalade, and although all the ingredients have to be bought you will find that home-made marmalade is far superior to (and less than half the cost of) shop marmalade.

I have included three recipes for jellies in this section—all of them are made with wild fruits, and all are delicious with meat or cheese. I have quoted no yield for these recipes but, as a rough guide, you can take it that for every 1 lb (480 g) sugar used you will obtain about $1\frac{2}{3}$ lb (800 g) jelly.

I do not possess a sugar thermometer, but get on quite well with my jam and jelly-making by guesswork. (It is all a question of allowing sufficient liquid to evaporate from your boiling jam. If it is runny when cold you probably have not boiled it long enough.) I stir my jam frequently when boiling, and when it loses that 'sloppy' look and drags against the spoon in a tacky sort of way, I know that it is time to take it off the heat. A traditional method of finding the setting point of jam or jelly is to drop a small amount on to a saucer and allow it to cool. If it wrinkles when pushed gently with a finger it is allegedly ready. In my experience, however, this is no more than a guide that your jam is coming up to the setting point. If you remove it from the heat as soon as this wrinkling occurs you may find that your finished jar of jam will not set.

Lemon curd is, perhaps, an anomaly in this book. I know that you can find jars bearing the label 'Lemon Curd' in your supermarket for which you will pay less than the price of the lemons, sugar, butter and eggs to make it yourself. But homemade lemon curd is so exquisite that I can't resist making one or two jars each year, and at least I know that the ingredients are pure and nourishing.

Now, with home-made sauces and chutney you can't

180

go wrong. Have you ever read the list of contents on a jar of supermarket chutney and wondered why such a long list of fruit, vegetables and spices also needed such items as 'edible starch, acetic acid, glucose, saccharine, flavouring and colouring'? Make it yourself and you will have pure food at half the cost! Although the only chutney recipe I have quoted is 'green tomato', you will find that almost any fruit can be turned into chutney in a similar manner and it will keep indefinitely. Chutney, in fact, improves with keeping.

Although syrups should be used up within three months, and jam will lose its flavour slightly after a couple of years, you should expect your preserves, that you have laboured over so long, to keep well. And at the risk of boring readers of my previous books I am going to repeat here a tip which, if followed, will ensure the keeping quality of your preserves. It is entirely a question of vacuum sealing them in sterile jars—and you don't need to buy jars or vacuum seals because they come free with most brands of honey, jam, peanut butter or pickles available to-day. (If you don't buy these products yourself, then scrounge the jars and lids from your friends who do.) Examine the lids of these jars. You will find that most of them have a plastic seal bonded inside. If this seal is undamaged then the lid can be used time and time again. First of all wash the jars thoroughly, then rinse with cold water. Do not wipe them. (A perfectly clean tea towel is still liable to leave bits of fluff behind.) Place them on a metal tray and put them into an oven with a low heat. After 20 minutes increase the heat slightly so that when you take the jars from the oven (which should be at the time your preserving pan is lifted from the heat) they are really hot. The lids of the jars should, in the meantime, have been washed, rinsed (but not wiped) and put into a pudding basin. Just before you are about to use them, pour boiling water over them. Now, lift your hot jars one at a time from the oven; fill each one with your preserve and, with tongs, lift out its lid from the basin and slap it on to the jar. Grab a tea towel and screw the lid on hard, and put to one side. As the jar cools, so the vacuum will form. (Incidentally, jars which have previously contained pickles or chutney should be used only for similar vinegar-based preserves. No matter how well washed, the jars are liable to remain tainted.)

It is not, in fact, strictly necessary to vacuum-seal jams or jellies in this way (if setting point has been reached and the correct proportions of sugar used they should keep satisfactorily)—but it is advisable to sterilize the jars by the oven method just described.

These jars with sealable lids—so kindly provided by the manufacturers of commercial preserves—can also be used with total success for bottling fruit. Wash and rinse the jar; pack it with the cleaned fruit, and fill to the brim with cold water. Place your jars on a metal tray and place in an oven with a low heat. Gradually increase the heat (over a period of time not less than 45 minutes) until the water in the jars is simmering. Leave to simmer for 2 or 3 minutes then remove the jars, one at a time, from the oven and slap on the lids that have been made sterile in the manner described above. I have never had a failure preserving fruit in this manner. (Jars which previously contained pickles can be used to bottle beetroot. Pack the jar with the sliced beetroot and fill to the brim with cold vinegar—then proceed as before.)

279. Mixed Fruit Jam (Summer Jam)

Makes about 3 $\frac{1}{2}$ lb (1 $\frac{2}{3}$ kg)

8 oz (240 g)
  blackcurrants
8 oz (240 g) redcurrants
8 oz (240 g) raspberries

8 oz (240 g)
  strawberries
2 lb (960 g) sugar

Simmer blackcurrants in 4 tbsps water until soft. Add all other fruit and simmer for 5 minutes. Stir in sugar and continue stirring until dissolved. Bring to a full rolling boil and continue rapid boiling (stirring occasionally) until setting point is reached. Remove from heat, allow to cool for a few minutes then (using a small jug) pour into hot sterile jars and cover immediately.

280. Wild Fruit Jam (Hedge Jam)

Makes about 6 $\frac{1}{4}$ lb (3 kg)

8 oz (240 g) sloes, or
  wild plums
8 oz (240 g) rose hips,
  chopped
8 oz (240 g) haws
8 oz (240 g)
  rowanberries

8 oz (240 g) elderberries
2 lb (960 g) crab apples
1 lb (480 g) blackberries
4 oz (120 g) hazelnuts,
  chopped
3 $\frac{1}{2}$ lb (1 $\frac{2}{3}$ kg) sugar

Simmer sloes, rose hips, haws, rowanberries and elderberries in 3 pts (18 dl) water for about 1 $\frac{1}{4}$ hours, then pour into jelly bag to drip into pan overnight. Next day tie the peel and cores of crab apples in muslin bag and put into the pan, together with apples, blackberries and hazelnuts. Bring to the boil and simmer until fruit is soft. Remove muslin bag, then add sugar, stirring continuously until dissolved. Bring to a full rolling boil (stirring occasionally) and continue rapid boiling until setting point is reached. Remove from heat, allow to cool for a few minutes, then (using a small jug) pour into hot sterile jars and cover immediately.

281. Wild Blackberry Jam *Makes about 3 ½ lb (1 ⅔ kg)*

2 lb (960 g) blackberries *2 lb (960 g) sugar*
1 lemon

Simmer blackberries with juice of lemon (and pips tied
in a muslin bag) in 4 tbsps water until soft. Remove
muslin bag and add sugar, stirring continuously, until
dissolved. Bring to a full rolling boil and continue rapid
boiling (stirring occasionally) until setting point is
reached. Remove from heat, allow to cool for a few
minutes, then (using a small jug) pour into hot sterile
jars and cover immediately.

282. Alan's Favourite Marmalade (chunky)
Makes about 3 ½ lb (1 ⅔ kg)

1 lb (480 g) Seville *2 lb (960 g) demerara*
  oranges   *sugar*
1 lemon

Simmer fruit in 2 pts (12 dl) water until skins are soft
(when skins can be easily pierced with a matchstick).
Remove fruit and leave to cool. Chop into chunky pieces
and remove pips. Put fruit back into the pan of water
and add sugar. Bring to the boil and simmer, stirring
continuously, until sugar is dissolved. Bring to a full
rolling boil and continue rapid boiling (stirring occasionally) until setting point is reached. Remove from
heat, allow to cool for a few minutes, then (using a
small jug) pour into hot sterile jars and cover
immediately.

283. Aunt Daisy's Carrot and Lemon Marmalade
Makes about 3 ½ lb (1 ⅔ kg)

2 lb (960 g) carrots,   3 lemons, halved
  grated   2 lb (960 g) sugar

Squeeze juice of lemons into bowl and mince peel. Add peel to bowl of juice, together with pips tied in a muslin bag. Add 1 pt (6 dl) water, cover with a cloth and leave overnight. Next day simmer with carrots until peel is soft. Remove muslin bag and add sugar, stirring continuously until dissolved. Bring to a full rolling boil and continue rapid boiling (stirring occasionally) until setting point is reached. Remove from heat, allow to cool for a few minutes, then (using a small jug) pour into hot sterile jars and cover immediately.

284. Mother-in-law's Marmalade (minced)
Makes about 3 ½ lb (1 ⅔ kg)

1 lb (480 g) Seville   1 lemon, halved
  oranges, halved   2 lb (960 g) sugar

Squeeze juice of oranges and lemons into bowl and mince peel. Add peel to bowl of juice, together with pips tied in a muslin bag, and 2 pts (12 dl) water. Cover with a cloth and leave overnight. Next day simmer until peel is soft. Remove muslin bag and add sugar, stirring continuously until dissolved. Bring to a full rolling boil and continue rapid boiling (stirring occasionally) until setting point is reached. Remove from heat, allow to cool for a few minutes, then (using a small jug) pour into hot sterile jars and cover immediately.

285. Lemon Curd — Makes about 1 lb (480 g)

2 lemons
4 oz (120 g) butter

8 oz (240 g) sugar
2 eggs, beaten

Melt butter in a thick-bottomed saucepan over a very *low* heat. Stir in sugar, juice and grated rind of lemons. Continue stirring and when runny add eggs, slowly. (If mixture goes lumpy, remove from heat immediately, beat briskly, then return to heat.) When mixture begins to thicken, pour into hot sterile jars and cover immediately.

286. Quick Candied Peel

4 oz (120 g) quartered
   orange or other
   citrus fruit peel with
   pith removed to leave
   only a thin layer

4 oz (120 g) sugar (plus
   a little extra sugar)
1 tsp bicarbonate of
   soda if a soft peel is
   required

Place peel (and bicarbonate of soda if desired) in a saucepan. Pour boiling water over and soak for 20 minutes. Drain, rinse peel, then bring to the boil in $\frac{1}{4}$ pt ($1\frac{1}{2}$ dl) water and simmer (with lid on) for 20 minutes. Stir in sugar, bring to the boil, then remove from heat and leave overnight. Next day gently bring to the boil and simmer over a very low heat (with lid off) until a little of the syrup forms a hard ball when dropped into cold water (about 20 minutes to 1 hour). Remove peel and place on a sugared plate. Pour remaining syrup on to the peel (or use to flavour custards, milk puddings, etc.). Store peel in jars when set and cold.

287. Rose Hip Syrup *Makes about 2¼ pts (13½ dl)*

This is good with milk puddings.

2 lb (960 g) ripe rose   *1 lb (480 g) sugar*
hips (wild or garden),
minced

Drop rose hips into 2 pts (12 dl) boiling water. Bring back to the boil quickly then remove from heat and leave for 15 minutes. Pour into jelly bag to drip into pan overnight. Next day put pulp into 1 pt (6 dl) boiling water, bring back to the boil quickly, remove from heat and leave for 10 minutes. Pour into jelly bag to drip into first lot of juice for a few hours. Bring juice to the boil and simmer until reduced to about 1½ pts (9 dl). Add sugar and boil for 5 minutes, then (using a small jug) pour into hot, sterile jars and seal immediately with sterile lids. Keep in the dark and use within 3 months.

288. Hawthorn Jelly

This is good with cold meat or cheese.

about 4 lb (2 kg)   *1 lb (480 g) sugar for*
hawthorn berries   *each pt (6 dl) berry*
                            juice

Simmer berries in 2 pts (12 dl) water in a saucepan (with lid on) until soft. Mash in pan, then continue simmering for 10 minutes. Pour into a jelly bag to drip into pan overnight. Next day add sugar (as above). Bring to the boil, stirring frequently until sugar is dissolved, then bring to a full rolling boil and continue rapid boiling until setting point is reached. Remove from heat, allow to cool for a few minutes, then (using a small jug) pour into hot sterile jars and cover immediately.

289. Rowanberry Jelly

This is good with hot roast pork or lamb, or any cold meat or cheese.

about 4 lb (2 kg)
  rowanberries
juice of 1 lemon for
  each pt (6 dl) juice

1 lb (480 g) sugar for
  each pt (6 dl) juice

Simmer rowanberries in 1 pt (6 dl) water until soft, then pour into jelly bag to drip overnight. Next day add lemon juice and sugar (as above). Bring to the boil, stirring frequently, until sugar is dissolved, then bring to a full rolling boil and continue rapid boiling until setting point is reached. Remove from heat, allow to cool for a few minutes, then (using a small jug) pour into hot sterile jars and cover immediately.

VARIATIONS

Bitter Rowan Jelly: For a sharper jelly use only 12 oz (360 g) sugar for each pt (6 dl) rowanberry juice.
Rowan and Ginger Jelly: Add 1 tsp ground ginger to each pt (6 dl) rowanberry juice

290. Elderberry and Crab Apple Jelly

This is good with cold meat or cheese.

about 2 lb (1 kg)
  elderberries
about 1 lb ($\frac{1}{2}$ kg) crab
  apples, chopped

1 lb (480 g) sugar for
  each pt (6 dl) juice

Simmer apples in 1 pt (6 dl) water until soft, then add elderberries and continue simmering until they are soft. Then follow method used for Rowanberry Jelly (previous recipe), but excluding lemon juice.

291. Elderberry Relish   *Makes approx. $\frac{3}{4}$ pt (4 $\frac{1}{2}$ dl)*

This is good with cold meat or cheese.

about 1 lb ($\frac{1}{2}$ kg)
  elderberries
about 8 oz ($\frac{1}{4}$ kg) onions,
  chopped
$\frac{1}{2}$ pt (3 dl) vinegar

2 oz (60 g) Barbados
  sugar
1 tsp mixed spice
$\frac{1}{2}$ tsp ground ginger
a pinch of salt

Gently simmer elderberries and onion in $\frac{1}{4}$ pt (1$\frac{1}{2}$ dl) vinegar until soft, then press through strainer or sieve to remove seeds. Return purée to pan with all other ingredients, bring to the boil and gently simmer, stirring continuously. When mixture begins to thicken remove from heat, allow to cool for a few minutes, then (using a small jug) pour into hot sterile jars (or wide mouthed bottles) and seal with sterile lids immediately and place in a pan of simmering water for 30 minutes (to ensure sterilization).

292. Tomato and Apple Sauce
               Makes approx. 1 $\frac{1}{2}$ pts (9 dl)

1 lb (480 g) red
  tomatoes, skinned
  and chopped
1 lb (480 g) cooking
  apples, cored and
  chopped
2 oz (60 g) onions or
  shallots, chopped
1 clove garlic, chopped
4 oz (120 g) sugar

$\frac{1}{4}$ pt (1 $\frac{1}{2}$ dl) vinegar
1 tsp cayenne pepper
1 tsp salt
spices tied in muslin
  bag:
  1 tsp allspice berries
  12 black peppercorns
  6 cloves
  2 chillies
  2 pieces root ginger

Gently simmer tomatoes, apples, onions and garlic in a saucepan (with lid on) until soft, then add all other ingredients and simmer (with lid on) for 30 minutes. Rub through sieve and return purée to pan. Then follow method used for Elderberry Relish (previous recipe).

293. Green Tomato Chutney   *Makes about 8 lb (4 kg)*

about 5 lb (2½ kg) green
  tomatoes, sliced
1 lb (480 g) onions,
  sliced
1½ oz (45 g) salt
8 oz (240 g) apples,
  cored and quartered
8 oz (240 g) sultanas
4 oz (120 g) raisins
4 oz (120 g) currants
1 clove garlic
2 pts (12 dl) vinegar

3 tsps mixed spice
1 tsp cayenne pepper
spices tied in muslin
  bag:
  6 tsps allspice berries
  1 tsp black
    peppercorns
8 chillies
7 cloves
4 pieces root ginger
1 lb (480 g) Barbados
  sugar

Put a layer of tomatoes in a large basin, cover with a layer of onions and sprinkle with salt. Repeat layers (until all tomatoes and onions are used) finishing with salt. Leave overnight. Next day mince with apples, dried fruit and garlic. Turn into preserving pan with 1½ pts (9 dl) vinegar and all spices. Bring to the boil and simmer until tomatoes and onions are soft and nearly all liquid evaporated (about 2 to 2½ hours). Remove muslin bag and squeeze into pan, then add sugar and remaining vinegar, stirring continuously until sugar is dissolved. Continue simmering until as thick as desired, then (using a small jug) pour into hot sterile jars and seal immediately with sterile lids.

Note: The quantities of fruit and spice quoted happen to be those used the last time I made this chutney. Any combination may be used—according to your taste, or what you happen to have. Garlic may be omitted and other fresh fruits may be substituted for apple. The dried fruits and spices need not be those specified, but the quantities (or proportions) given should not be drastically altered.

294. Tomato Ketchup

Makes approx. 2 pts (12 dl)

2 lb (960 g) red
   tomatoes, skinned
   and chopped
¼ tsp cayenne pepper
spices tied in muslin
   bag:
    1 tsp allspice berries
    8 black peppercorns
    7 cloves

3 chillies
¾ pt (4 ½ dl) vinegar
8 oz (240 g) cooking
   apples, peeled, cored
   and chopped
4 oz (120 g) onions,
   chopped
3 oz (90 g) sugar

Simmer spices in vinegar for 10 minutes. Gently simmer tomatoes, apples and onions to a thick pulp, stirring continuously. Rub through sieve and return purée to pan. Discard bag of spices and add vinegar to purée, together with all other ingredients. Then follow method used for Elderberry Relish (recipe no. 291).

10. Miscellaneous

This section contains all the oddments that didn't seem to fall under the previous headings . . . and the oddest of them all is, perhaps, Brwyes (recipe no. 302). A concoction of dripping, bread and hot water may not be your ideal breakfast, but Eirlys P. (who gave me the recipe) considers it to be a staple food. And if, like her, you started each winter's day clattering about with ice-cold buckets on the frozen muddied cobbles of a remote hill farm, you too might be glad to know that a bowl of Brwyes was keeping hot for you on the side of the fire.

Eirlys farms alone, living on a primitive holding that only recently was connected to the main electricity supply, and her name will live forever in the folklore of these parts as the woman who took on MANWEB

(Manchester and North Wales Electricity Board) single handed, with defiance and a chain saw.

When MANWEB brought electricity to the area Eirlys was persuaded to allow their poles to cross her land on the promise of a free installation of power to her farm. She was a bit put out when she discovered that the electricity itself wasn't going to be free—and she was absolutely incensed by the 'standing charge'. She refused to pay it. Over a period of eighteen months MANWEB tried persuasion and threats to no avail. When they sent in the men to disconnect her supply Eirlys was ready for them. With chain saw in hand she confronted them in her muddy little yard. 'You cut off my electricity and I'll cut down your poles!' Ten of these poles marched in a straight line over her land. She could have felled the lot in an afternoon. MANWEB's team considered the situation . . . (angry little women waving chain saws wasn't an every-day situation for them) . . . and retreated.

I would like to have recorded the fact that Eirlys won. I would like to have said that MANWEB, intimidated into submission, had admitted defeat; but I can't. In the end, worn down by constant bullying and cajoling, Eirlys capitulated. She now pays her standing charge—grumbling—like the rest of us.

What has all this got to do with the section of miscellaneous recipes? Nothing. I just wanted to tell you about Eirlys.

295. Plain Pastry

This is suitable for pasties and flans. It can be rolled very thin and the finished cooked pastry will not fall to pieces if held in the hand to eat cold.

3 oz (90 g) margarine (or   *8 oz (240 g) plain flour*
butter, or beef
dripping)

Rub fat into flour. Add water to make soft dough.

296. Short Pastry

This is suitable for all pies, tarts and baked puddings.

2 oz (60 g) margarine (or butter)	vegetable cooking fat, or beef dripping)
2 oz (60 g) lard (or	8 oz (240 g) plain flour

Chop all fat into flour with a knife until lumps are no more than pea size. Add water to make firm dough.

297. Suet Pastry

This is suitable for all dishes with pastry, baked or boiled.

4 oz (120 g) suet, fresh-chopped (or packet)	8 oz (240 g) plain flour

Mix suet with flour. Add water to make soft, pliable dough.

298. Daisy's Tasty Snacks

any raw pastry scraps	a little yeast extract (or grated cheese)

Roll pastry very thin to oblong, spread a little yeast extract or cheese over. Roll widthwise and seal edge. Cut roll into slices and lay each 'wheel' upon a lightly greased baking sheet. Bake in a hot oven until crisp and brown (5 to 10 minutes).

299. **Dumplings** (savoury and sweet variations)

BASIC SAVOURY

5 oz (150 g) self-raising   2 $\frac{1}{2}$ oz (75 g) suet
   flour   a pinch of salt

Mix ingredients together then add water to make soft dough. Then, with floured hands, form into balls about 1$\frac{1}{4}$ in (3 cm) in diameter. Cook in rapidly boiling soup, stew or casserole for about 20 minutes.

VARIATIONS

Onion dumplings: Add 1 chopped shallot and $\frac{1}{2}$ tsp mixed dried herbs.
Curry dumplings: Add $\frac{1}{4}$ tsp curry powder and a dash of Worcestershire sauce.
Cheese dumplings: Add 1 oz (30 g) grated cheese and 1 tbsp chopped chives.

BASIC SWEET

Omit salt and add 1 tbsp sugar. Form into balls about 2 in (5 cm) in diameter. Cook in rapidly boiling water and serve with custard sauce, chocolate sauce, syrup or jam.

VARIATIONS

Chocolate dumplings: Add 1 tsp cocoa and a few drops vanilla essence.
Coconut dumplings: Add 2 oz (60 g) desiccated coconut and a few chopped glacé cherries.
Currant dumplings: Add 1 oz (30 g) currants and $\frac{1}{2}$ tsp mixed spice.

300. Baked Suet Crust (Mendip Pudding)

SAVOURY

Use the basic dumpling mixture (recipe no. 299) or one of the savoury variations, and spread in a shallow, ovenproof dish. Bake in a hot oven for about 20 to 25 minutes. Serve with meat and vegetables, etc. (Like Yorkshire pudding, this is used as a 'filler'.)

SWEET

Use one of the sweet variations of the dumpling mixture (recipe no. 299) and bake as above. Serve with custard sauce, chocolate sauce, syrup or jam.

301. Potato Dumplings

8 oz (240 g) boiled potatoes, mashed	$\frac{1}{2}$ oz (15 g) butter
1 egg, separated	1 tsp yeast extract
1 $\frac{1}{2}$ oz (45 g) wholemeal flour	pepper

Beat white of egg until stiff. Mix together all other ingredients thoroughly then fold in white of egg. With floured hands form into balls about 1 in (2$\frac{1}{2}$ cm) diameter. Drop into rapidly boiling soup, stew or casserole and cook for about 15 minutes.

302. Stale Bread Gruel (Brywes)

This is a traditional Welsh breakfast dish.

2 tbsps breadcrumbs	salt, pepper
1 tbsp oatmeal	$\frac{1}{3}$ pt (2 dl) boiling water
1 tsp dripping	

Mix together all ingredients.

SWEET VARIATION: Omit dripping, salt and pepper. Use hot milk instead of water and add chopped apple, a little dried fruit, a few chopped nuts and a sprinkle of sugar.

303. Mixed Herb Stuffing

1 tbsp chopped fresh
   sage or 1 tsp dried
   sage
2 tbsps chopped fresh
   thyme or 1 dsp dried
   thyme
2 tbsps chopped fresh

marjoram or 1 dsp
   dried marjoram
6 oz (180 g) onions,
   grated
5 oz (150 g)
   breadcrumbs
salt, pepper

Mix together all ingredients.

304. Mint Stuffing

3 tbsps chopped fresh
   mint or 1 tbsp dried
   mint
1 tbsp chopped parsley
5 oz (150 g)
   breadcrumbs

3 oz (90 g) onions,
   grated
1 tbsp milk
salt, pepper

Mix together all ingredients.

305. White Sauce (savoury)

1 oz (30 g) butter
1 oz (30 g) plain flour

salt, pepper
$\frac{1}{2}$ pt (3 dl) milk

Melt butter in a saucepan. Remove from heat, then stir
in flour to make smooth paste. Add seasoning and the
milk gradually, stirring continuously. Return to gentle
heat, stirring until the mixture thickens.

306. Special Cheese Sauce

3 oz (90 g) cheese,
  grated
$\frac{1}{2}$ oz (15 g) butter
3 oz (90 g) onion, grated
3 oz (90 g) tomatoes,
  skinned and chopped

1 egg, beaten
3 tbsps milk
cayenne pepper
1 dsp chopped chives

Melt butter in saucepan and fry onions, tomatoes and cheese gently for a few minutes. Stir in egg, add milk and cayenne pepper, stirring continuously until thick. Remove from heat and add chives.

307. Quick Salad Cream

1 $\frac{1}{2}$ oz (45 g) butter
2 dsps plain flour
$\frac{1}{2}$ pt (3 dl) milk

2 tsps sugar
$\frac{1}{2}$ tsp salt
4 tbsps vinegar

Melt butter in a saucepan; remove from heat and stir in flour to make a smooth paste. Gradually add milk, then stir in sugar and salt. Return to heat and cook gently, stirring continuously until thick. Remove from heat and gradually beat in vinegar.

308. Jam Sauce

4 oz (120 g) jam

2 tsps cornflour

Make a thin smooth paste with cornflour and water. Stir jam into $\frac{1}{3}$ pt (2 dl) water and gently heat. Stir in cornflour paste and slowly bring to the boil, stirring continuously, until sauce thickens and clears.

309. Orange or Lemon Sauce

1 small orange or lemon
1 oz (30 g) sugar

1 dsp cornflour
1 tsp margarine

Grate orange or lemon peel, then squeeze juice into $\frac{1}{4}$ pt
($1\frac{1}{2}$ dl) water and stir in peel and sugar. Make a thin,
smooth paste with cornflour and water, then gently
heat juice mixture and stir in margarine, then cornflour paste. Bring to the boil, stirring continuously,
until sauce thickens and clears.

310. Butterscotch Sauce

$\frac{1}{2}$ oz (15 g) butter
4 oz (120 g) golden
  syrup

1 dsp custard powder
a few drops vanilla
  essence

Boil golden syrup until much darker in colour then
remove from heat. Make a thin smooth paste with
custard powder and water, then add $\frac{1}{3}$ pt (2 dl) water to
the golden syrup and reheat. Stir in custard paste and
bring to the boil, stirring continuously, for 10 minutes,
then add butter and vanilla essence and stir well.

311. Egg Custard Sauce (Sandra's Custard)

1 egg, beaten
1 tbsp cornflour
1 tbsp sugar
$\frac{3}{4}$ pt ($4\frac{1}{2}$ dl) milk

Suggested flavourings:
nutmeg, or vanilla
  essence, or cocoa, or
  orange juice

Mix egg, cornflour and sugar to a smooth paste in a
basin. Heat milk, pour on to paste, stirring continuously to avoid lumps. Return to saucepan, bring to
the boil, stirring continuously, and continue cooking
for a few minutes until thick, then stir in flavouring.

312. Mock Marzipan

Use as a topping or filling for cakes.

1 oz (30 g) margarine, or butter

2 oz (60 g) caster (or granulated) sugar

2 oz (60 g) semolina (or soyabean flour)

1 tbsp water

1 tsp almond essence

Put margarine and sugar into a saucepan and heat gently until runny. Then stir in all other ingredients—adding almond essence last. Work all together to make a smooth paste.

313. Hazelnut Filling (for cakes)

3 oz (90 g) hazelnuts, ground or finely chopped

2 oz (60 g) sugar

1 oz (30 g) breadcrumbs

juice and rind of half lemon

$\frac{1}{4}$ pt (1 $\frac{1}{2}$ dl) water

Mix all ingredients together in a saucepan and cook gently for a few minutes, stirring occasionally. (The consistency of the mixture can be altered by adding more water or more breadcrumbs, as desired.)

THE END

Index

All numbers refer to recipes, not pages

A SELECTED LIST OF AUTOBIOGRAPHIES AND BIOGRAPHIES AVAILABLE FROM CORGI BOOKS

THE PRICES SHOWN BELOW WERE CORRECT AT THE TIME OF GOING TO PRESS. HOWEVER TRANSWORLD PUBLISHERS RESERVE THE RIGHT TO SHOW NEW RETAIL PRICES ON COVERS WHICH MAY DIFFER FROM THOSE PREVIOUSLY ADVERTISED IN THE TEXT OR ELSEWHERE.

☐	12698 5	**Transit Point Moscow**	G. Amster & B. Asbell	£2.50
☐	12851 1	**Childrens Hospital**	Peggy Anderson	£3.95
☐	09332 7	**Go Ask Alice**	Anonymous	£1.95
☐	99054 X	**Borstal Boy**	Brendan Behan	£3.95
☐	99065 5	**The Past is Myself**	Christabel Bielenberg	£3.50
☐	12712 4	**Island of Barbed Wire**	Connery Chappell	£2.50
☐	09373 4	**Our Kate (Illus.)**	Catherine Cookson	£2.50
☐	11772 2	**'H' The Autobiography of a Child Prostitute and Heroin Addict**	Christiane F.	£2.50
☐	12727 2	**Men**	Anna Ford	£2.95
☐	12501 6	**Beyond the Highland Line**	Richard Frere	£1.95
☐	13070 2	**Born Lucky: An Autobiography**	John Francome	£2.95
☐	12833 3	**The House by the Dvina**	Eugenie Fraser	£3.95
☐	99098 1	**Autumn of Fury**	Mohamed Heikal	£3.95
☐	99158 9	**Brendan Behan**	Ulick O'Connor	£2.95
☐	99143 0	**Celtic Dawn**	Ulick O'Connor	£4.95
☐	99247 X	**The Ford of Heaven**	Brian Power	£3.50
☐	12577 6	**Place of Stones**	Ruth Jannette Ruck	£2.50
☐	13058 3	**The Marilyn Conspiracy**	Milo Speriglio	£2.50
☐	12589 X	**And I Don't Want to Live This Life**	Deborah Spungen	£3.50
☐	12072 3	**Kitchen in the Hills**	Elizabeth West	£2.50
☐	11707 2	**Garden in the Hills**	Elizabeth West	£2.50
☐	10907 X	**Hovel in the Hills**	Elizabeth West	£1.95
☐	99097 3	**Catch a Fire – The Life of Bob Marley (Illus.)**	Timothy White	£3.95

All these books are available at your bookshop or newsagent, or can be ordered direct from the publisher. Just tick the titles you want and fill in the form below.

TRANSWORLD READERS' SERVICE, 61–63 Uxbridge Road, Ealing, London, W5 5SA

Please send a cheque or postal order, not cash. All cheques and postal orders must be in £ sterling and made payable to Transworld Publishers Ltd.
Please allow cost of book(s) plus the following for postage and packing:

U.K./Republic of Ireland Customers:
Orders in excess of £5; no charge
Orders under £5; add 50p

Overseas Customers:
All orders; add £1.50

NAME (Block Letters) ....

ADDRESS ....

....